A Season of Life

A True Story of
Faith over Fear
Triumph over Tragedy
Repentance that led to Redemption

J.L. Tipton

DEDICATION

I dedicate this book first and foremost to God of creation. He is the one whom all great things come from and He is not limited in what He will do for us. It is entirely because of what Jesus died for on the cross that I am able to write this book today. I dedicated my life to God and everything I am able to do for the Kingdom I give back to God first.

Secondly to my Husband "the Crazy Preacher" Tim Tipton who has encouraged me to write since the moment I married him. He has stood by me in my pain and joy and in my frustration of completing this book. I love him and thank him for his devotion and vision to see good things I me that God wanted to use all along. I love my husband and "my" Crazy Preacher.

I also dedicate this book to my parents because they are the reason I am in this world and am alive today to share not only my story but to give glory to God.

My prayer is that as you read this that you will not look at the tragedy as much and instead will see the fingerprints of God. And that you will learn to know the difference. I also dedicate it to a great friend and author Kim Bettes who not only inspired me but showed me the way to get started and publish my story to share with the world.

I dedicate this finally to you the reader.

It is because God inspired me to tell my testimony to help anyone struggling with abuse, drug addiction, depression, self-esteem, suicide, anger, and unforgiveness.

Thank you for investing in this book and thank you for your contribution to helping to end hunger in our communities. Each book you purchase helps to buy a 105 lbs.' of food to feed the communities as well as homeless from Southeast Missouri to Northeast Arkansas and parts of Illinois, St. Louis, Springfield, South Arkansas and Texas. So, I am saying thank you to all who have helped to show love and support not only for me but for the thousands of people this book will help and feed both spiritually and physically.

SEASON'S

"The word which came to Jeremiah from the LORD, saying,
Arise, and go down to the potter's house, and there I will cause thee to hear my words.
Then I went down to the potter's house, and, behold, he wrought a work on the wheels.
And the vessel that he made of clay was marred in the hand of the potter: so, he made it again another vessel, as seemed good to the potter to make it."
Jeremiah 18:1-4
-KJV-

"The Cracked Pot"

God found me alone and weeping this morning and He gave me a word today about the Potters' Hands and the Clay.

He said; "You, my child are a fine work from MY hands why do you weep so?"

I said, "Because I have no beauty left. It's all scars of my life."

He said, "Yes child, that were once wounds. Did I not heal those wounds?"

"Yes, Lord you healed them."

"Then why do you still weep?"

"Because the scars left marks upon my body...who would ever want me now? Who would understand my hurts, my losses and my pains? Who would ever really see the beauty in me?"

He said "I Will my child."

He took my hand and led me to a throne room and I could hear trumpets resounding and angelic melodies. I heard joyous laughter and praise and I could see beautiful lights and colors surrounding the worshippers and He asked me, "Do you want to see where this comes from?"

I said "Yes Father."

He gently took my hand and led me down a path that brought me to a KING! His head was bowed before God and when He raised His head to look at me I saw GLORY! His eyes were soft, yet piercing in color brightness and royalty... a great love shone through... a PURE and COMPASSIONATE love I had never known or experienced before now. He smiled and stretched out His hands and as I stared at the wounds in His nail scarred hands, the man who sat on the throne... I knew... He was MY KING!

I bowed before Him and He invited me to visit with Him. As we visited for what seemed like a long time yet not long enough... He told me the truth of His nail scarred hands. I began to weep harder now and hung my head in shame.

He said, "My child, why are you weeping? Do you not know how the Father loves you? Do you not know you were created with the Masters Hands? He is the Potter who created you and when the sin of life tried to destroy you and crushed your body, bruised your spirit and whipped you... I stood in the gap!" "You were put on the altar of MERCY and GRACE... and there while you rested and the Potter worked on you to heal your body and create in you a new spirit of truth and righteousness, while you rested in Him ... I stood in the gap." "Do you not know, my child, my scars were for you?"

I looked up at Jesus in awe of His beauty, and I knew then what He was trying to show me. It was only through the scars that Gods beauty and glory could bring forth His beautiful light! It was at the work of the Potters Hands that He indeed healed me and worked wholeheartedly to mold me to be stronger than before so that I could hold and carry what He had for me and could withstand many trials that I would still face.

(2Co 4:6) For God, who commanded the light to shine out of darkness, hath shined in our hearts, to *give* the light of the knowledge of the glory of God in the face of Jesus Christ.

(2Co 4:7) But we have this treasure in earthen

vessels, that the excellency of the power may be of God, and not of us.

(2Co 4:8) We *are* troubled on every side, yet not distressed; *we are* perplexed, but not in despair;

(2Co 4:9) Persecuted, but not forsaken; cast down, but not destroyed;

We may look at ourselves as a "cracked pot", something no one could ever love...But we are created by God in love and through love and He is the true artist of us!

A true artist can make something beautiful and unique out of nothing and call it an original!

God makes us beautiful and unique and creates in us His light... His ORIGINAL light!

He creates a match for us as well... One who will love us unconditionally, even with scars, sickness and things the world considers defective!

Never cover up the scars of life that you may bear on your flesh or in your spirit...instead, let Gods light and Glory shine through them...

Remember it was the brightness of the star that led the wise men to Jesus, let that brightness in your scars lead all men to God!

Do not be afraid...God has glazed you with HIS love and with FAITH! Therefore, there is no room for the spirit of fear of who will love you or accept you!

When you search for and learn who the true Potter is, then and only then will you know who YOU ARE!

One final thought... Had it not been for the scars in OUR KING... we would never understand nor clearly see the beauty and greatness of TRUE LOVE... of HIS LOVE!!

IT'S GREAT TO BE A CRACKED POT...BECAUSE I KNOW I BELONG TO THE POTTER!

This is a true testimony of my life. To protect the people involved I have left their names out of this book.

This is my story

Unto the woman he said, I will greatly multiply thy sorrow and thy conception; in sorrow thou shalt bring forth children; and thy desire shall be to thy husband, and he shall rule over thee.

And unto Adam he said, Because thou hast hearkened unto the voice of thy wife, and hast eaten of the tree, of which I commanded thee, saying, Thou shalt not eat of it: cursed is the ground for thy sake; in sorrow shalt thou eat of it all the days of thy life;

Thorns also and thistles shall it bring forth to thee; and thou shalt eat the herb of the field;

In the sweat of thy face shalt thou eat bread, till thou return unto the ground; for out of it wast thou taken: for dust thou art, and unto dust shalt thou return.

Gen 3:16-19

–KJV–

"Birthing Pains"

Time sure fly's by when you're not looking. As a child we always think and really believe the days never seem to end and that twelve years of school is a whole lifetime. But as we get older and finally become adults we are awakened to the reality that our life passed by more quickly than we thought and yet strangely what happened forty or fifty years ago seems like only yesterday.

I guess there are certain things we keep closer in our memory both good and bad that alter time in our minds.

It's a good thing we can't remember back to when were born. For instance, the day I was born, my dad said I was his miracle baby because of the situation that surrounded my purpose of being in this world.

When my mom found out she was pregnant with me she was also informed that she had cancer in her ovaries and cervix and the doctors said it would be a tragedy to attempt to carry a baby to term. It would be a death sentence for me anyway.

They thought my mother was crazy because she refused to have an abortion and knew we might both die, but God was holding us for sure. My mom hemorrhaged during my birth on August 28th 1965 and had an extended hospital stay, we both lived and I was a plump eight-pound baby girl.

Happy and Healthy and blessed as could be. Mom had to stay in the hospital and after much surgery and sixteen pints of blood she was finally on the road to recovery.

My Dad was immediately attached to me and me to him. He said from the moment I became a part of life here, I didn't cry like most babies do when the doctor gives them a whack on their bottom to get them using those lungs. Instead I opened my eyes and smiled at the first person I saw and that was my dad. We had an immediate bond.

My dad has always said that God had a special plan for my life and he knew that it was something really special because the devil fought too hard too destroy me and didn't stop with trying to take me out before I ever came into this world. When that didn't work he tried something new because you see the devil doesn't give up so easily but neither does God.

The day came to get my first set of baby shots and something in them made me really sick.

The doctors thought I had contracted the virus that they were giving me the shot for, so they gave me a shot of penicillin to make me better but after I got home I had a really bad reaction to the antibiotic and my dad found me in my crib not breathing and blue. I was rushed to Los Angeles Children's Hospital and fell into a coma and stayed there for the next fourteen months. Both my parents took turns watching over me and praying.

The Doctors saw little hope, but my dad believed I had a strong will to live and a mission in this life to accomplish for God. He never lost hope or faith in what God was doing while I was in a place of rest for those fourteen months. I was 18 ½ months old when I opened my eyes and ironically it was once again my dad that I laid eyes on. Only God could plan that perfect timing. From that day on it was as if nothing ever happened to me. I played like a normal baby and rarely ever cried about anything. I was happy and I had wonderful loving parents. I remember my mom so well; she and I were together all the time and I loved doing everything with her. If she was writing a letter and she did every day, I would sit beside her and scribble on paper a letter too and she would always send it with the letter she wrote. I copied everything she did and I loved her so very much. I was her little side-kick of course, until dad came home, then I was a daddy's girl!! I had lots of brothers and sisters and I just thought we were a happy family, but I guess just because everything seems great on the surface does not mean there isn't some kind of a war going on behind the shadows. And in that war my mom left me when I was only four years old and that changed everything in my world forever.

When we become adults, we forget what the world to child looks like and that it is both beautiful and scary. So, when a parent leaves and pulls the family apart a child is not just affected but completely unearthed, uprooted and afraid. If one parent leaves then the other might leave too.

From that day forward, I was terrified of everything especially people. I was withdrawn and shy and emotional and sad because I missed my mom and I didn't understand why she would go away.

She took everyone but me. So, I went on growing up believing my dad was the only person who must really love me. As I was reaching the age of five I knew my dad was troubled and worried about me having a mother to teach me the things I needed and I could tell It was a lonely time for my dad too.

Even as young as I was, I felt hurt for him.

I saw his pain and part of that pain was that he

wanted me to have a mom. I imagine he felt it would be hard to bring up a little girl all alone.

One day he just came out and asked me if I wanted a new mom. I told him I wanted him to be happy.

I felt if my dad was happy, then I was happy because nothing else mattered to me.

He had met a lady and I thought she was beautiful and she had a son a year older than me so that meant I might have a brother again since my real mom took all the kids with her and then left them to raise themselves.

I spent some time with this new to-be mom and she seemed really nice.

PARENTS: To kids, having someone to love them and show them affection is a BIG deal!

And that is something I hadn't had from a mom figure in almost a year which was too long for a child.

I knew my dad was so in love with her and I wanted him to be happy.

So, on February 2nd 1971 my dad got married. He got a new wife and I got a new mom and another brother and things seemed to be perfect!

ALMOST...

Things aren't always what they seem.

Two weeks after they got married the gate to hell opened and my world shook and never stopped shaking after that.

"Children shouldn't have to sacrifice So that adults can have the life they want.

You make sacrifices so your children can have the life they deserve."

Author Unknown

"Sacrifice's"

My step mom had a drinking problem and a pill problem. She would drink beer all day and eat valiums while my dad was at work. She told me up front that she was not my mother but I would do whatever she told me to do. She punished me for everything that she could think of. She was angry or depressed all the time. She was always beating on me with whatever she could find but her favorite was the Sears catalog. (In those days they were huge)

She would lock me in my room with no food or water for sometimes a day and sometimes longer if my dad was gone, having to work double shift's. She said I could stay there till my dad came home so that may be a few days. My new step-brother would sneak boiled eggs under my door and I would hide in my closet and eat them.

She loved him because he was her son, but he wasn't anything like her. He was my best friend!

We never told my dad that she was hitting me because it seemed like they had problems of their own.

See by the time my dad got home from work, my mom was drunk, and in a rage and would be cussing my dad.

My dad would put on old country music (Hank Williams) and pop open a beer and start trying to be light heart-ed and really trying to woo her but it just made her more violent.

She would throw knives at him and one time I remember she pulled a rifle out and shoved it in his stomach and pulled the trigger.

My step-brother had unloaded it when she

wasn't looking. Thank God because it would have killed my dad.

My dad is a good man and no matter what he faithfully read his Bible and taught us from day one about God.

He tried his best to teach us about the Love of God and it stuck in  some ways and in other ways it seemed like how could God really love us if He was letting us stay in this hell? But my dad continued to love us and teach us about God every chance he had and because of that love I had of God early on, I taught myself to read my Bible and I was actually reading on my own at the age of four.

It is because of what my dad taught me that I fell so in love with God!! I would talk to Him and Jesus all the time.

I would chase the clouds to find Him...run outside in a storm and dance in the rain with Him.

As I let the winds wrap themselves around me I

would imagined I was being carried by angels.

God was my only way out and my only way in and even as much as I thought I knew Him I was too young to understand how true that was.

I was never taught about salvation. I did know how to pray fervently and I did with all my heart. I would cry out several times a day and pray for Him to forgive my mom for being so mean and I asked God in my prayers to keep my heart soft and to never let me be mean and to help my mom and my dad.

I know God heard me. I just know He did...

But if He was really listening, where was He?

Why wouldn't He rescue me?

Why was it okay for me to go through all of that and no one would help me?

I didn't understand, but I kept holding on to God.

As time passed, after being locked up, locked out, beat, and cursed by my step mom, life was no longer normal for me. I was always in and out of hospitals with my kidneys trying to shut down, and I hated being at home and especially alone with her.

My dad and her fought all the time. sometimes they fought so bad they would beat each other really bad and the cops would get called. My brother would get taken to our aunt and uncles house or to his dads' house, but my dad wouldn't let me leave because I think he was scared they wouldn't bring me back.

When my real mom left me she actually came back one day and kidnapped me, I don't remember any of it and I am glad I don't. I don't think she kidnapped me because she really wanted me since she wasn't able to raise me or my brothers and sisters. I would have ended up in the foster system much like them or living on the streets like my sister was put. It's a shame how kids become on the losing end of the parent's sin.

Anyway, my dad called the police and state police and got a judge to sign full custody of me over to him and together with all that a man hunt started and they searched four states before they found me and got me back.

From that day on my dad became so over protective of me that it was ironic to me that he would marry a woman with so many mental issues that would hurt me. But I guess he really didn't know.

Sometimes in life we can be so desperate for something that is missing in our life, that we try too hard to go after the wrong thing believing it's the best decision.

I wonder where my life would have been like if none of this would have happened? All the things I could have grown up to be and do changed in this moment, because from this moment everything in my life would become a curse.

My step mom hated my real mom and called her horrible names to me all the time. She would yell at me and tell me I was a whore and would end up just like my mom.

I was only five years old. It broke my heart to see all the hate and anger and how I felt the cause of it, as if somehow what my mom had done was all my fault.

I wanted to see my real mom so badly and one

day I went snooping through my dad's desk drawer and found all the pictures he was saving for me of my mom and my brothers and sisters and old projector films also of all of us together.

I remember finding a picture of my mom holding me as a baby she was so beautiful and I took it to my step mom and said "See here is my mommy, she isn't a whore she is a mommy and she is pretty and she does love me." My step mom became so enraged and demanded I take her to where I had found the picture and I did. She grabbed the drawer out and threw everything in a pile in the back yard and burned it and made me watch. I cried and cried. That day burned a horrible hate in my heart.

No matter what I did to try to make her happy and love me she didn't. She never favored me at all in anything.

I remember one instance she had given my step brother some money to go to the store and buy candy and a soda. In those days you could buy a whole bag full of candy and a glass bottle coke for a quarter. Anyway, when I asked her if I could have a quarter you would have thought I asked for the bank.

She yelled at me and screamed

"Do you think money grows on trees?"

"Get out of my sight and don't ask me for anything again!"

I told her "well yes money could grow on trees if God wanted it to."

With that she slapped my mouth and I ran out of the house crying. I went and hid by an old Buick we had in the yard and cried and prayed to God.

As I was crying my brother came to see what was wrong and I told him. He said "sis, I believe if you asked God to make money grow on trees and He wanted it to He would make it happen."

I was so happy he had faith I asked God for some money and at the moment I asked the wind blew and a twenty-dollar bill came falling out of our old oak tree. The surprise on our faces I am sure to God was priceless!

We ran in to show her that yes God makes twenty-dollar bills grow on trees. Needless to say, I got beat for it.

No matter what I would never belong to her and she would never have a heart for me to love me as her child.

I knew this for a fact.

As the years passed It just seemed like everyone was either fighting over me or blaming me for their problems.

Don't get me wrong we had some happy days. every family does even if it's for an hour of the day, it's still a day or a moment that something was actually good.

We took family vacations like normal families, which were wonderful because we would be gone for weeks at a time and it would be in those weeks that my parents never fought. We actually laughed, sang songs, told jokes and had a made some great memories.

We barbecued, had family get-together's and even went to the Kingdom Hall once in a while

Yes, my parents professed being Jehovah's

Witnesses when in reality they rarely ever even went to a meeting, they were too embarrassed by their lifestyle and my step mom was Catholic so she wasn't really interested in my dad's religion she just went anyway.

They really were an odd couple and toxic for each other. And honestly, I didn't know a lot about the downside of my dad's beliefs until I became an adult.

However, at that time in my life, our religion didn't matter to me because those were the best times. Times I felt normal and thought God had answered my prayers to have my family healed.

But like all other days, those days too would end...

The sun would go down...

and the gates to hell would open up again...

Oh, how I wanted to disappear.

J.L. Tipton

WRITE DOWN SOME OF THE THINGS YOU WENT THROUGH AS A CHILD THAT MAY BE KEEPING YOU FROM MOVING AHEAD

What is causing all the quarrels and fights among you? Isn't it your desires battling inside you?

2 You desire things and don't have them. You kill, and you are jealous, and you still can't get them. So, you fight and quarrel. The reason you don't have is that you don't pray!

3 Or you pray and don't receive, because you pray with the wrong motive, that of wanting to indulge your own desires.

James 4:1-3

-CJB-

"Discord"

We had moved several times and no matter where we moved it didn't change our life inside. I remember my dad moving us and lying to the realtor about why all the windows had been broken out. He told the realtor that some kids did it, because the truth was too horrific and embarrassing to tell.

My step mom had gone into a drunken rage and busted out every single window in our house with her hands. It was a terrible and frightening night for me and my brother, we stayed hid in our room playing our record player as loud as we could to drown out all the horror that was going on.

No matter where we moved, nothing could make our house a "Home Sweet Home." We all knew this but the move always seem to make the past seem farther away from us and we were able to look forward a new tomorrow before it became blemished with horrible memories.

This time we moved hours away which would be good because nobody would know us and we could get a new start with new friends and a new school. I was getting better at hiding the hell that was going on at home and the bruises from even my best friends.

We moved to Houston, Texas in a really nice suburban neighborhood with lot of families which meant kids to hang out with. There me and my brother had our own rooms that were right next to each other so I felt safer just knowing he was only a wall away. We immediately ventured out in the neighborhood and made friends with the kids. A few of them became best friends and lifelong friends I am thankful for. I knew the secret life inside our house couldn't stay a secret here, there were to many people around. That thought alone gave me a glimmer of hope.

I loved being in the city. There were so many more activities to stay busy in to keep me away from home. I swam a lot and eventually joined the swim team. I played softball, played the flute in band, and was a cheerleader. I loved staying busy it made me feel that was what "normal" felt like to other kids. And my mom actually got a job at a local dry cleaners and went to work every day.

My dad was a manager for a one of the largest grocery store chains in the area and was on television every Sunday on the Don Mahoney and Jeana Claire Show because the grocery company was one of their biggest sponsors and they used my dad to represent the company.

So...

We looked to most to be the normal suburban family and it seemed we were becoming that. But as always, in the bottom of a beer can that all changed. It was a "dark and stormy night" after that. Before long the neighbors knew how our lives were and it was so embarrassing.

We eventually moved from there too and lived in an apartment complex for a couple of years. It was pretty tame there. No real fighting and if there was fighting, it wasn't long before the police showed up at our door. So, they behaved pretty good.

It was at this time in my life that God was doing some wonderful things in me as far as gifts are concerned, and in a one day sitting I discovered I could write upside down and backwards in cursive.

I was so excited about it and thought if my parents could see how intelligent I was, that maybe my step mom would love me and wouldn't tell me anymore that all I was ever going to be was a whore like my mom. If only they could see.

So, I wrote my dad an entire letter and handed it to him. He looked at me and said, "what in the world is this?" I told him "turn the paper around and upside down, Dad". When he did he was amazed.

He asked me where I had learned this at and I told him "nowhere dad it just happened." He was so excited he took it to my step mom and well the next thing I knew I was sitting in a Psychiatrist office looking at an old Russian doctor who was reading my letter I had wrote my dad.

He kept looking back at me and said in a long groaning voice." hmm''." hmm," and put down the letter.

He wrote some things on a pad and handed it to me.

It read: "YOU ARE INCREDIBLE!"

I smiled at the doctor and it was then he told me all about how most people only use one side of their brain but I use both sides. That I was blessed with an extraordinary gift. I was so excited and in the back of my mind a little defensive toward my parents especially my step mom thinking, "see I told you I'm not crazy and I'm not a whore either".

But I just sat quietly and listened as the doctor explained all this great stuff to them.

CAUTION: Whatever you call a your child will be imparted in their mind forever. Speaking good or bad things determines how a child will view themselves as adults.

When we left I thought I would hear some

sort of praise or an "I sure am proud of you". But instead I heard my step mom say, "well he doesn't know what he is talking about!" I thought "man and you paid him a hundred and fifty dollars to not know what he is talking about!" I just couldn't win for losing so I gave up trying.

A year later we finally moved into a house outside the city limits and well the houses were set further apart so my parents could argue and fight all they wanted.

I hated living with them and I hated my life and I had already begun to hate my step-mom. I was depressed all the time and I really wanted to die or run away. My dad worked all the time and instead of coming home he went to the night-club's and little bars and drank until he was drunk enough he thought to be able to handle the hell at home with my mom. But it was horrible, they would have knock down drag out fights waking us up and I was just tired of it all and I wished I could just leave.

It wasn't until my dad ended up in bad car wreck that he began staying home more and drinking.

I will never forget that night waking up to the banging on the door. It was the police and they had come to let us know my dad was in a very bad accident.

He was drunk and passed out stopped at a traffic light and two teenage girls who were also drunk and driving too fast didn't see his lights and the light had turned green so they sped up doing 60 mph and rear-ended him knocking him through the intersection.

The doctors said it was a good thing he was passed out or his injuries could have been deadly.

So, my dad went to court and had to pay a fine and I am not certain of all the details I just know he stopped going to the bars and I was happy that he did.

I often wondered what would have happened had he been killed.

What would my life be like then with a mother who couldn't stand me and didn't   know how to be a mother to me.

Where would I end up?

The thought scared me.

After the accident, things changed. My dad was home more and I thought again that things might get better and actually some days seemed better but if they both started drinking it was nights of fighting and cussing and arguments.

By now my step brother had already moved out and went to live with his real dad soon after we moved into the new house, so there was no one for me to turn to anymore.

I started making friends in the neighborhood and got introduced to pot and hash and acid. It was fun once in a while but I really didn't like being that way even though it was a way to escape the truth of homelife. I also learned early on that the fun is only fun until someone gets hurt.

One night that happened as my friends and I were high on acid and I got in the car with them and we ended up in a terrible car wreck leaving the girl that was driving totally paralyzed and mentally impaired and me and the other girl pretty banged up.

I never did acid again and never got in another car with someone high on acid and somehow was able to keep it from my dad and step mom.

Not that they would notice anyway, after all I stayed away from home as much as possible because when I was home my step mom was crazier than ever.

She was back taking valiums and mixing them with whiskey, vodka and beer and she would become violent and tear up the house and if I was in it she would take that violence out on me.

I wished I was somewhere else.

"Be careful what you wish for.
I know that for a fact.
Wishes are brutal,
unforgiving things. They
burn your tongue the
moment they're spoken
and you can never take
them back."

-Alice Hoffman

"Wishing"

One day my wish came true. I wished I was somewhere else and the events that took place the day before took me right out of that house and my parents' custody over me.

The night before this happened, my stepmom in one of her crazy fits beat me so badly that I couldn't hide the bruises and when I got to school my coach saw me and literally cried and picked me up and carried me like a baby to the office. He was a big guy and a tough coach who was a really very softhearted man. Of course, the school called the police, child protective services and my dad.

They had a big legal meeting and told my dad he would have to get me out of that environment or I would be put in foster care and then into the system.

Texas is a no-nonsense state when it comes to child abuse even to this day.

I felt sorry for my dad that day because he really was clueless and naive about things or I just hid it really well or they were too caught up in their own drama to take notice to what their drama and her abuse was doing to me.

I know many people today tell me that shame on my dad for not protecting me and partly they are right but partly they have no idea about my life and what I allowed to be known and what I hid in secret.

My step brother and I never told my dad never all the things she did to me because we were afraid he would hurt her or even kill her. We were scared kids we didn't know what would happen really but we weren't going to take the chance to find out either. There would be no gain having lost both parents.

My dad was all I really had left.

After CPS (Child Protective Services) and the police released me to my dad with the legal agreement that he would have to take me to my grandparents to live because that day they were granted custody of me until I was eighteen.

My dad decided I would need my things and we would have to go back to the house and pack my things.

NOT A GOOD IDEA...

Supposedly the police had come to the house to arrest my stepmom but they didn't tell us when they arrived she wasn't there.

They were looking for her though.

They didn't know she had hidden in the attic.

So, when we got there and got my things packed and started for the door she ambushed me and my dad hitting him with something and then kicking him until she kicked him so hard in the groin that he hit the ground. I ran to punch her and my dad screamed at me to get in the car. But I helped him up and started telling him we had to get out of there.

As he tried to get in the car and get his

composure she came out with a box cutter and slashed his arm and before I could do anything he was chasing after her towards the house and I knew if I didn't catch him he would kill her.

By the time I got to him it was too late.

It was horrible.

My dad had tried to grab her and instead in the middle of their fight he pushed her so hard she fell face first into the fireplace busting her head and her mouth wide open and there was just blood everywhere.

It was the worst scene ever, and one I have never forgotten even to this day.

I was horrified for her and for my dad and for the first time in my life I felt sorry for her and afraid. But there was no time to be afraid.

Before I could wrap my mind around what had just happened, my dad put me in the car and we took off towards my grandparents three and half hours away.

I was crying so hard and said we had to go back, but it wasn't any good.

I wasn't the adult and my dad he was terrified of losing me forever so we just ran.

As he drove neither of us said anything, my dad was shaking and only asked me if I was okay and he kept apologizing.

I cried until I eventually fell asleep.

I had no idea that along the way again our lives would be put in danger and this time not at the hands of my step mom but at the hand of my dad.

After I fell asleep my dad had stopped and bought a fifth of whiskey and I imagine he drank it pretty fast. Fast enough to get rid of the pain, all the horrible thoughts racing through his mind and evidently which direction we were supposed to be traveling because I woke up to the sounds of sirens not only behind us but surrounding us, because we were we driving towards traffic and headed straight for two 18-wheelers.

All I saw was lights coming right for us.

The officers surrounded our car boxing us in until my dad ended up back in the median and then the Sherriff opened the door and began to reach in for my dad.

That is when the fear in me grew into rage and I screamed and bit the Sherriff and began crying and punching him so he wouldn't take the only parent I have left away from me.

My dad was so drunk he was just slurring his words and giggling telling me to "stop and behave". But I didn't.

I kept trying to fight for him.

But they took him anyway.

The Sherriff was a kind and gentle man. He scooped me out of the car and held me like he was my own dad.

And I held on to him as tight as I could.

And I cried.

I cried until I passed out.

It was still really late when we got to the place where I would now be living.

I guess the sheriff and his wife were really good at loving kids because they had a whole house full of kids they had adopted and were fostering some and had some of their own too.

They were wonderful people and, in the year, I lived there I really began to love them.

BUT...

I missed my own dad.

I knew I wasn't going to get to go back home because the court had ordered that I would be in the custody of my grandparents.

Once again, the fight was because of me and now again it was a fight over me.

I couldn't wait to just grow up.

After the whole incident with the police, my dad sat in jail for months.

My step-mom got put in a mental institution for a long time.

And I was taken to my grandparents to live.

I couldn't believe this was the result of my wish.

Fear thou not; for I am with thee: be not dismayed; for I am thy God: I will strengthen thee; yea, I will help thee; yea, I will uphold thee with the right hand of my righteousness.

Isaiah 41:10

–KJV–

"A New Day"

I was afraid and nervous even though I loved my grandma and grandpa with everything in me. They were such loving people and so much so it almost seemed too good to be true. But I couldn't imagine they would love me very long. Somewhere down the line they would find fault with me and wish I would leave.

I was always waiting for the hammer to drop, but it never did. It was then I knew I was finally safe.

My grandma was such a great mom to me and she helped me to cope with all the bad things by praying with me, reading me the bible and just loving me. I went to a new school where no one knew me and I loved the fact that for once I had a normal home life.

I made friends and made first chair flute and my grandparents came to every function our school had that included me in it.

My grandparents were so very poor. They really couldn't afford another mouth to feed but they were happy to have me there and it showed.

My grandpa was an East Texas logger his whole life and his retirement gave him fifty dollars a month to live on. It wasn't much at all but they never let it affect them.

They had their own little farm and a huge garden that they tended by hand.

They traded produce for milk and meat and grandma made butter, soured milk and cottage cheese. And the best homemade biscuits and tea cakes you ever had.

We had farm fresh eggs and it was my job to collect eggs every morning at 3:30 am and I loved collecting the eggs. But, I didn't like the mean old rooster that chased me every morning.

But it was worth it to smell eggs and bacon and sausage cooking, biscuits in the oven and the smell of percolated coffee brewing and listening to my grandma sing praises to God as she cooked.

I had chores in the morning and after school chores as well, "normal chores", Like helping grandma with hanging out laundry and washing dishes, beating out rugs and sweeping. Then there was the "farm chores" like boil and feather a hen that was not laying eggs anymore so we could have a nice dinner, working in the garden, harvesting vegetables for dinner and cleaning them. And feeding the animals and making sure the pens cleaned and were locked up tight for the night.

Then it was time for homework.

My grandparents were also Jehovah's witnesses and I and was expected to go to the Kingdom Hall whenever there was a meeting. I didn't mind any of it because this was so much better than the life I had been having to live.

I remember I would watch my grandparents

just talk to each other and they never argued.

I watched not only how they treated each other but also how they treated my aunts, uncles and cousins and thought how in the world did my dad not see the evil in this woman he married? He was raised in a home with so much love.

I guess love is blind when it comes to the worldly desires.

The difference is what you chase after.

If you chase after God you will know and live and experience real true love and relationships of real love.

But if you chase after the desires of the world you will find grief and false hope.

My grandparents did a wonderful job with me and I will never forget how my grandpa took his entire fifty dollars one month and as he handed it to my grandma he whispered something in her ear.

Later I found out what it was.

He had given her his whole check to take me shopping to get me a pretty dress and shoes for my junior high graduation. (I was a smart kid, a straight A student and was moved up grades when I was in elementary school, so I was always younger than my peers.)

I didn't know what to say.

Since my grandma and my aunt sewed all their own clothes why would they take me to buy something out of a store.

I think it as the first time I learned not only the value of a dollar but the true love my grandparents had for me and my love for them. I was more worried about their survival than having something pretty to wear.

I didn't want them to spend their only means of support on me and after we laughed and made deals, I finally caved and agreed only if we went to k-mart because I knew it was the cheapest store around.

For twenty dollars I got a new dress, a fancy pair of shoes, a pair of pantyhose and a necklace too. And my grandparents got to save the money that was left.

I'll never forget how much they loved with sacrifice.

The day of my junior high graduation came and I was excited because my dad was coming to see me and I couldn't wait.

But what happened next, I didn't expect.

He had gotten a special weekend pass for my step mom to come out of the hospital and see me graduate.

There were so many things I didn't understand back then and literally not until after I got saved.

So, I was really angry.

I didn't realize, know or even really care what she did while she was committed in the hospital.

I didn't know or care that she was going through therapy.

None of that mattered to me because I hated her.

I did not want her in my life or my dad's life.

And yet here she was...

At my graduation.

That night after my graduation ceremony my step mom handed me a gift that she had special made just for me.

A sterling silver bracelet that had charms from every sport I had ever been in.

And as she handed it to me she told me how proud of me she was.

That was something I never heard.

I wanted to hang on to that forever.

I remember looking at her lip and her head and still seeing the scars that had set in so deep. It made my heart hurt so bad for her. I knew there must be some deep scars I couldn't see also, and it was if the hate and anger I had held in for so many years, suddenly like a flood drained right out of me and I cried and hugged her.

I felt so bad that she had been hurt so bad and nearly died that day. And for the first time in many, many years I felt love for her.

The evening ended well and the visit the next day was good too and then my dad left to take her back to the hospital and I remember asking him when I would get to see him again but he didn't know.

In that moment, I realized how homesick I was and for some crazy reason I missed my step mom too.

They left and I felt sick...

I became so depressed...

I couldn't seem to overcome it...

It paralyzed me.

WRITE DOWN THE BEST MEMORIES OF YOUR GRAND PARENTS and YOUR PARENTS THAT YOU CAN REMEMBER

8 We have all kinds of troubles, but we are not crushed; we are perplexed, yet not in despair;

9 persecuted, yet not abandoned; knocked down, yet not destroyed.

2 Corinthians 4:8-9

-CJB-

"A Dark Summer"

The summer was here and I should have been excited but I was still so depressed and homesick. I called my dad every day and begged him to let me come back home. But he was afraid because of the court system, that if he got caught that he would never get to see me again.

My grandparents came up with a plan that if my dad would move, they would change their mailing address to my dads' home and that way I could live with him even though they would be three hours away, we could make it work.

My dad came and got me and we had moved into a mobile home he was buying, he sold the other house and we lived in really nice trailer park until the end of the summer. That's when we moved completely away from Houston and into the country. An hour and a half away.

Yes, this was going to be perfect, just me and my dad finally.

I thought.

I was still battling with depression and now anxiety because my dad still worked in Houston and I stayed home by myself in the country miles from civilization.

He went in before I went to school and he didn't get home until I was already in bed. So, it was as if I was living totally alone and I was lonely. When the weekend would come I would get my hopes up that we would go do some things together, but he was always worn out from working so hard and wanted to be home.

I had way too much time to think about things and the more I thought the more I wanted so badly to find my real mom and see for myself what she was like and if she really loved me. But my dad didn't want me to find her, he said it would be more trouble in our lives and we didn't need that.

I couldn't understand though why he wouldn't let me meet her. I just felt like my life had been turned upside down again and I couldn't get over being severely depressed. I had never been so scared and lonely as I was then.

I wanted to die.

So enough was enough and one evening when my dad was at work hours away I wrote him a letter telling him why I was ending my life.

That evening I tried to take my life by drinking a fifth of my dad's vodka, eating a bottle of Tylenol and cutting myself.

I figured one of them would kill me even if the Tylenol failed. It didn't work.

God works in mysterious ways.

My dad had a bad feeling in his heart that whole day and called sent one of my best friends and her mother to come surprise me and they found me passed out in my bedroom floor and bleeding. After that night my dad called the sheriff and they found my real mom.

Let your father and your mother be glad, and let her rejoice who gave birth to you.

Proverbs 23:25

-KJV-

"Forsaken Dreams"

I thought for sure that when I saw my real mom that somehow my life would magically transform into a Cinderella story. And that my real mom would be happy to see me, to know I loved her and I was okay.

I have to be honest here, everything I imagined my mom to be, was from stories my family would tell me of how beautiful she was and how loving she was. So that is how I imagined her.

However, when she stepped off the plane into the terminal, I looked at every woman coming off the plane and never saw anyone who could be my mom.

The last woman to get off the plane was a heavy-set middle-aged woman with big bouncy bleached hair and lots of makeup on and I saw her smile at my dad with a flirty smile and I wanted to run.

This woman was not my mom!

She came up and walked right past me, hugged my dad and gave him a kiss on the cheek and she smelled like cigarettes and alcohol and I was just devastated.

I never spoke those thoughts until his moment.

I didn't care that she was overweight or that she was bouncy. I just knew she was a honky-tonk woman like my step mom had crudely said all these years that she was.

She never gave even gave me a hug.

She was more interested in talking to my dad then meeting her daughter.

My heart was shattered and I wanted her to go away.

When we got home, my dad told her he found her not for him but for me. So that she could get to know me and maybe have a relationship with me.

My Dad had rented her a place where I could be with her and that last about three weeks.

She was never home, always at the bars after work and bringing old bar drunks' home.

I hated her so much that I remember the last time I saw her I threw an 8-track stereo at her and told her to go back where she came from.

I called my dad and he took me home.

What a great disappointment. I had been trying to identify with my family. To figure out if there was anything good in me worth loving. All I saw was the same old stuff and I didn't like it.

It made me really hate who I was.

I already had real self-esteem issues and now that I had met her I realized even more that didn't want to be like my real mom because she wasn't a good person.

My dad was a broken vessel too.

A Season of Life

Oh, my what kind of person was I then?

I hated my life.

Hated it.

Hated everything about it.

And where was God now?

I continued living with my dad and I was happy but manically depressed too.

I began hanging out with some of the known drug dealers in the area. We lived in the country and there are more drug dealers living in the country than in the city.

These guys adopted me as their little sister. And I felt protected. They didn't let me use or even drink because I was just a kid and they didn't want that for me. And I hung out with them every day.

Somedays they would take me to the lake and fish and swim and other days they were racing cars. It was during this time I realized how much of a tom-boy I really was and I loved racing cars too.

I knew how to drive and every chance I got I was behind the wheel.

One day I got busted by my dad, he came home early from work only to run into me with the car on two wheels rounding a 15-mph curve on a gravel road. He was so terrified he swerved and ran his car into the ditch. I was terrified to and all I saw was his face red and mad in the rearview mirror. I got the car down on all four wheels and came to a stop. I was shaking but I was excited and I jumped out of the car and said "Dad. Did you see that? I won!"

He didn't share in my excitement or my victory.

I was grounded. After all I was only 13.

My dad didn't like that I was hanging out with them but there wasn't a lot he could really say. He worked almost two hours away and left me home by myself all the time.

And after a while he knew they would always protect me, more so than he ever did.

I think my dad was really noticing my life was going in a direction that he no longer had control over because he spent too much of my life putting too many other things first.

Mainly work.

Don't get me wrong, I know my dad had to work, but he was addicted to his job. I also believe his work became his life for so many years so he wouldn't have to come home to the hell house. Whatever his reasons were then, didn't mean they had to be that way now.

After all it was just me and him.

Did he not want to be around me? I never told him how confused that made me feel.

One day my dad came home from work to have a "talk" with me and asked me what I thought about my step mom coming back home and us all giving things another chance.

I was terrified in some ways and in another odd way I really missed her.

I agreed under one condition, that they promise to not drink.

Not even once.

I don't know why I believed they could hold that promise, but it was my one condition.

A week after she was released from the

hospital they got drunk and had an argument and she took a stoneware plate full of food and busted it across my dad's head knocking him out.

I punched her and knocked her out too.

I went and packed two suitcases full of clothes.

I left that night walking down a mile-long sand road in the middle of the dark woods looking for which direction to go and I didn't have any idea where that was but I didn't look back either. I was scared but the things that went on in my house were way more frightening than the things going on in the dark woods.

The only thing I left them was a note that read;

"I am done with living here in your mess. I am leaving and I am not coming back so don't send the law or try to come looking for me or I will tell everyone what you both have done!"

I was done!

"Know ye not that they which run in a race run all, but one receiveth the prize?"

"So run, that ye may obtain."

1 Corinthians 9:24

-KJV-

"A Time to Leave"

That night I got to the end of that mile-long road and I sat down on my suitcase in the dark.

There were no cell phones in those days so it wasn't like I could call for help. But I did have a way to contact a friend I hadn't talked to in a long time.

God.

I prayed and began to cry and once again, I felt totally alone and afraid.

I asked Him to help me find my way. In the middle of that prayer I heard a man's voice and it was the man who lived where I was sitting. He asked me if I wanted to come in and I told him "no thank you". But he insisted. He went back inside his house and brought his wife out to get me. I was shaking uncontrollably and I knew I wanted to just go far away, but where?

I had met a young man a month before who was older than me but I really had a crush on him. I had no idea he was friends with these people's son. But he was and he came over while I was there and said I could come stay with him and his mom.

His mom was a nurse and he explained how his mom actually knew me and really liked me.

This was so embarrassing and totally awkward for me but what other choices did I have at that moment?

Sleep in the woods?

No, I couldn't do that.

There were too many dangers there too.

I had to drop my fear of everything and make an adult decision.

For the next few days I stayed with this boy and his mom until I could figure things out. His mom took me down to the courthouse to speak to the judge that she was really good friends with and after talking to him about how things were, he granted me my freedom. I could live on my own as long as I worked and stayed in school and showed I could be a responsible young lady.

That same week I got my first real job sacking groceries at a little grocery store, I moved in with one of the cashiers that worked there and we shared rent and utilities and we got along great. I was keeping up with my grades and I got my permit at 13 ½ and then my hardship license at the age of 14 and my driver's license at 15.

I really liked the boy that helped me and was totally smitten by his smile and his big blue eyes. He was two years older than me so I couldn't date him until I was older, it just wouldn't be right. And there was one thing I still could salvage about my life was my reputation as a young lady. I was saving myself for my husband.

When I turned 15 we started dating and on my 16th birthday we got married in a cute little church ceremony.

I thought this is my second chance to have a normal life. The life I pictured and planned, nothing like my parents lived!

Young women have an idea of life and marriage and family that they start planning out for themselves from an early age and they have this unrealistic image in their minds of who their husband is what he looks like and how perfect he is. Well that is a scary thought because young men are not thinking of those things or how they are going to be a perfect husband.

We all come with baggage that puts us in a position that we have to learn to live with each other's flaws which can be dangerous especially when your flaw is anger and violence.

My husbands flaw was just that!

I felt so destroyed inside because now my homelife was a whole new nightmare. No matter which direction I ran in this life I kept running into violence and the one being hit.

I had held in so much hurt and pain for so very long I knew one day I would self -destruct. What I wasn't paying attention to is that I was already self-destructing.

I quit high school in my junior year and at the time I really didn't care what anyone thought about it. I just stayed working and tried to be a perfect wife.

Perfection and Beauty do not change abusive people.

It wasn't long at all before I was being beat by the man who said he would love me forever.

I remember I was so insecure I didn't want to fail at my marriage, so I tried to be the picture of perfection for him and I became a victim of his anger problems.

The devil will deceive you in ways that it seems that things are perfect when really, it's a picture of perfection on top of a foundation that is rotten and it crumbles.

Every girl dreams of the perfect marriage and even if it isn't perfect she is relentless to make it perfect even if it means sacrificing your own happiness.

It is the one thing she is searching for...

I too did this...

I found myself married to a drug addict, adulteress, and abusive man.

I had fallen into the arms of the life I tried so hard to escape.

I left that marriage in fear and I ran far away.

But not far enough.

WRITE DOWN THE PLAN YOU HAD FOR YOUR LIFE

WRITE DOWN HOW LIFE TURNED OUT

"I have to find a place to hide

An island in the sea

Surrounded by a racing tide

Where I can live with me"

— Laurie Matthew, Groomed

"Vanishing Act"

After I ran away from my husband and my family I found myself moving farther away from everyone I knew. I enrolled in beauty school and I worked three jobs and did anything I could do to get that dream life and to erase my past. It was hard because it seemed so much had happened that had seared me and left me worthless and I just couldn't see a light at the end of the tunnel anymore. I thought maybe this would be my way to salvation but in reality, a lot of painful times were in store for me, my life was cursed.

It wasn't long before I was getting sick a lot and feeling weak and I went to the doctor to hear the news that I was pregnant. I didn't know what to do. How could I ever get away from my husband now? I'm going to have our child. He didn't know where I lived and I was thankful for that. I never have believed in abortion and I wasn't going to adopt my child out. I didn't know how I would manage this I was only 17.

As the months went on my belly grew bigger. I didn't go home to visit because I didn't want my dad and step mom to know. She would have done everything in her power to cause me to lose my baby and I wasn't taking that risk.

I was happy but I was alone.

I stayed in beauty school and I kept working three jobs my entire pregnancy.

I didn't know what I was having, I didn't even know I was carrying twins. But I was.

One night I heard a pounding on my door and when I looked out the peek hole I saw that it was my husband. Somehow, he found out where I lived.

Sweetly he asked me to let him in.

I opened the door and felt the blow to my head and then to my belly and then again to my head.

I don't remember anything after that.

I woke up in the hospital feeling like I had been hit by a truck and disoriented. I had no idea where I was how long I had been there or remembered why.

Until I touched my belly.

Where was my baby?

I been screaming and a nurse ran into help me and broke the news to me about what had happened.

That is when I found out I had twins and little boy and a little girl.

I was devastated beyond belief.

The grief a mother feels when she has lost her child is so heavy there is nothing that can lift that burden of loss. (Except God)

They sent the police in to speak with me and I pressed charges but remember the judge was friends with his mother and money can talk any language and it did. He won and I lost and now I was scared for my own safety!

I had no one to turn to

I didn't feel like anyone even cared about the hell I was going through, my marriage was cursed, I was in fear and "still" in what I thought was true love. I couldn't go home couldn't tell anyone what I was going through, because they would just tell me what a loser I was or wouldn't understand or would tell me I got what I deserved.

Everything just built up in me for way too long the thoughts racing through me so fiercely of all that had happened and what I had been through one tragedy after another...

and one day something in me snapped...

I ran again.

I loaded up a twelve pack of beer, my bible, a change of clothes and pain pills in my car and took off for South Padre Island, Texas. I had no clue where I was going and I had only about eighty dollars, no job or home to look forward to and I didn't know any a soul there.

I just left town and disappeared hoping no one would ever find me.

As I made the trip I drank one beer after another which alone took its toll on me quickly because before this moment I hated alcohol and had never drank beer before. But here I was driving drinking and then took some pills. The drive grew long and I grew tired and in a drunk and drug induced stupor I wrecked my car into the South Padre Island bridge.

I don't remember anything after that.

I woke up a few days later in a strange house with seven strange men there of all ages.

My first thought was oh no they have been raping me and I'm kidnapped and they're going to kill me. But they let me know I was safe and they cried tears of joy to know I was alive.

And they told me what had happened that night.

They saw what was happening on the bridge with me driving all over the place because they were beside me. When they saw my head drop they drove their car in front of mine to save me from going over the bridge. They got me out of the car to safety and got the cars off the bridge miraculously even before one cop showed up. They paid to get my car fixed and offered me a job in construction.

I took it.

I stayed there having my own room and paying my part to be there and I worked every day that was available. I was adopted in like a little sister to seven big brothers.

I was living a new life.

The Jaimie everyone knew was gone now and I was content because I figured if I was gone then no one in my family could blame me for their problems anymore.

Finally, some peace.

A year goes by quickly for some ...but a year burns like hell fire for a parent who has a missing child.

I missed my dad and I had no idea how much my dad was hurting for me not knowing what happened to me. My dad, had the FBI looking for me for a year and by a miracle they eventually found me.

They couldn't force me to come home but the man who found me was also a father and with tears in his eyes he asked me to at least promise to call my dad and let him know I was okay.

I called...

We cried...

We talked...

And cried some more...

And I agreed to come home to visit but I made it clear I wasn't going to stay.

When I got there, we had a nice visit and the night before I was to leave my dad took my car keys and drove my car to a lock up facility and hid it.

When I realized my car was gone I hit the roof. But I couldn't prove anything even when I called the police. (my parents' lived in a crooked little town) So I gave them a description of my car and they left.

But how was I going to get back to my home now?

I didn't know my dad had taken my car a hid it until almost a year later.

My dad owned a small business and asked me to come to work for him and I did. I really didn't have a choice.

I knew when my dad had asked me to come home to visit there was a bad feeling and I should have listened to it. But no matter what, inside I was just not truly happy anywhere and no matter how many times I ran away I just could not seem to find the happiness anywhere that I was searching for.

What I kept finding was manic depression and suicidal thoughts constantly overshadowing me, controlling my emotions. I just really didn't care or know how to care anymore.

I came home to my parents only to see the same junk in their lives.

Arguing, drinking, fighting and my name always being brought into the middle of it.

Nothing had changed...

I wasn't staying in that mess.

I worked hard and earned enough to start buying a house and I bought a new truck.

Just as everything was getting a little better I got hit with the worst news I could ever have heard.

"You Have Cancer"!

**WRITE DOWN THE THINGS OR SITUATIONS
YOU HAVE OR ARE STILL RUNNING FROM**

**WHAT MAKES YOU WANT TO RUN FROM
THEM?**

He said to them, "Because you have such little trust! Yes! I tell you that if you have trust as tiny as a mustard seed, you will be able to say to this mountain, 'Move from here to there!' and it will move; indeed, nothing will be impossible for you!"

Matthew 17:20

-CJB-

J.L. Tipton

"Mountain Climbing"

A year after I had moved back home I found out I had cancer. And it was not just going to the doctor and finding out. No nothing in my life happened that way. Tragedy always seemed to make a dramatic entrance with me.

My dad later told me the cancer I had was the same kind my mom had when she was pregnant with me. Ovarian and cervical and it was in my colon also.

However, by the time they discovered it I was already too far gone.

A Season of Life

When I think back I am amazed on how God ordained his steps in my life along the way.

No matter the tragedy surrounding me God was always right there in the middle of it holding on to me.

The day that the devil tried to again take me out, my aunt and I had gone to the mall to do some shopping, she knew I was depressed and wanted to get me out. As we were walking through the mall I noticed some young kids looking at me in horror and pointing. I looked at my aunt and we giggled a little until one young girl screamed "Oh my God she's bleeding to death"!

We all looked around to see who she was screaming about and then without warning, I felt the life draining out of me as I looked down and realized I was standing in my own pool of blood.

I was already hemorrhaging badly and was rushed to the hospital.

The first hospital I was taken to didn't have the capacity to help me and I was rushed to

Memorial City Hospital in Houston Texas.

As my parents were talking to the doctors and nurses I remember an older African American gentleman looked to be about 70 years old. He had the sweetest smile and a head of snow-white hair. I don't know what his name was but he came to me and said "sweet child let me get you in a room and out of this wheel chair."

They had me strapped in. I was so weak I knew my life was about to end. I agreed and he wheeled me to a room and he got me on a stretcher and he brushed my hair back away from my forehead and said "Child God has said His grace has always covered you but He is also not going to let anything happen to you. You will live and will be blessed". And he kissed my forehead and I felt peace and I let go.

(I will more about this man in my next book)

I actually had lost so much blood that I passed out.

When I woke up I was in an operating room and they were talking about my options. None sounded good at all. And They wanted to act right away with chemo and with the little strength I had in me I told them no way, that I would rather die. They were going to have to do surgery anyway and I would never be able to have kids again.

I was only eighteen years old and just couldn't believe what I could have ever done to receive so many terrible things in my life.

They had done a complete hysterectomy and taken out a quarter of my colon and I spent the next year in an incubated room.

I don't remember a lot about being in the hospital but I do remember waking up once to find my step mom blowing cigarette smoke into my incubated tent. I pressed the button and the nurses came in and she was banned from my room.

Back then they allowed smoking in the hospitals.

So, I stayed in the hospital for a year, I was crippled up and weighed a mere seventy-eight pounds when I was released.

I was supposedly cancer free. But now I would never walk again. My bones had constricted while I was in there and even with the mobility exercises they said they did with me while I was out, my body didn't respond to any of it.

From what I have learned and know now I know that my care was questionable.

So now the journey began...

I couldn't stay alone and I didn't have any insurance anymore, because back then "cancer" was considered a pre-existing condition, so the insurance company cancelled my policy and refused to pay my hospital bill that was $125,000.00 dollars.

So, after I was released I had to go stay at my parents' house and I still had to deal with my drunken step-mom because I had no one else to take care of me.

I felt like I was in prison, how did my life get to this?

Why was I even born?

So many times, I cried out "Why God, why won't you just take me off this earth?"

I was tired of fighting a losing battle.

Then one day God sent a God-fearing man and one of my best friends to come to my side who really came to help take care of me.

He would read me the Bible every day and

shared Godly values with me. I felt like God had sent me a protector.

His dad was a Methodist Preacher and because of his obedience to speak the WORD of God into my life I started going  to church and it felt really good. He even helped me learn to walk again not just in the physical but in all the other parts of my life too. It was as if God said I'm going to use him to help you get UP Jaimie, not give up.

We spent every day together and we fell in love even though I still had no clue what real love was but got married that spring anyway.

We were married nine years total but only together about half of that. He went into the Air Force and well the devil got to him and he began having affairs with the women in the service and outside of the service too.

I was devastated.

We kept trying to work it out only to realize we

were not any good at marriage. Not only that I battled with the loss of my babies and I wanted more children and I hated myself for not being able to give him a child.

He didn't want any children. But I did and worse than ever.

The doctor who had done the surgery for my cancer told me there is a time span they look at, that any cancers return usually happens within the first five years.

Well...

Five years later to the day, I ended up with cancer again.

I had been living in San Antonio Texas and my husband and I were separated so I was alone. I was at work when my kidneys were hurting and I couldn't stand. With my job as a hairdresser I had to stand. So, they sent me home for the day.

Within the hour of me being home I became violently ill. I had no one there and no we still didn't have cell phones and I didn't have a home phone either. So, I got up taking grocery bags with me to have something to get sick in and I drove the forty-minute drive to the nearest hospital.

When I arrived the security, guard helped me and got me into the emergency room. They let me set there for another hour as I got worse and by now was throwing up in mop buckets and couldn't stop. The emergency room was packed out but suddenly it was like I had the room to myself.

Guess that's what you have to do to get first class treatment.

They got me to a room and my kidneys began shutting down and I was rushed into an emergency surgery room. They had to put double -J stints in my kidneys because not only were they failing they were becoming enlarged. I was told that it could kill me.

The next morning, I was taken down for more tests. They came back and told me I was pregnant.

I laughed so hard I think I split a stint.

I explained to them that there was no way possible that I could be pregnant. I had a hysterectomy and I hadn't been with anyone because me and my husband were separated.

So, I told them check again.

Yeah, they did and found out the "pregnancy" was a tumor and cancer.

I was taken into surgery the next morning.

This time I only spent thirteen weeks in the hospital.

My husband didn't come to help me this time and we never got back together so we agreed on a divorce after Nine years.

But surprisingly the one person I never expected to see again in my life showed up.

My real mom.

She stayed a week with me and it was a better visit. We made up for the fight we had and we also talked about that I wouldn't expect her to be a "Mom" to me since she didn't raise me, but instead we would just learn to be friends.

That visit meant everything to me.

My Dad and step mom came to visit me for two days and one of those days the nurses let them sneak me out of the hospital to go to Sea World.

And there I got to pet Shamu.

I know most people would laugh about that. But the value of life was really starting to weigh on my heart. Seeing Shamu and being so close to tough him was like showing me the greatness of God.

As the days passed in the hospital I was really worrying deep inside about how I would be able to pay my rent and bills and my car note and if I would still have a job waiting for me.

One morning the nurse came in and turned on my television and said "Jaimie, you're not going to believe this."

One of my clients was on the news with a bunch of my other clients, they had gotten together to do a benefit for me and one of the major groceries stores donated meat and a whole bunch of stuff for a BBQ Benefit for me.

I was crying!

They raised enough money to pay my rent for a year, my car notes for a year and all my medical expenses. And I was offered a job in a high-end salon.

I couldn't believe the outpour of love from so many people. I stayed in San Antonio and worked there for another three years.

One day my dad called and asked me to come manage his business for him.

At first, I said "NO WAY!" Then he told me my step mom had cancer and it was bad and they needed my help.

So, I packed up my life and left my job and moved back to my little hometown.

By now my dad owned some rent houses and he had just purchased a beautiful little fixer upper and I paid $400.00 a month and worked on fixing it up in my spare time when I wasn't managing my Dads business.

My step mom was diagnosed with breast cancer and it wasn't a little lump it was a big one. It was really a bad time because they said it could have already spread. She was admitted into MD Anderson Hospital in Houston; Texas and they did a mastectomy on her.

Her healing time was horrible.

While she was in surgery they did some hypnotic thing where she would never want a cigarette again and would never want a drink again.

But her body was craving it and her mind was telling her she wasn't allowed to have it ever again.

So, she was hard to deal with but I helped her everyday anyway until the inevitable happened.

 One day she told me "you know all this is your fault, don't you?"

That was my last day over there.

She called everyone she knew and told them me and my dad gave her cancer.

It wasn't long before I moved too and quit working for my dad.

They were adults and I couldn't put my life through that anymore.

WRITE DOWN YOUR MOUNTAINS THAT YOUR CLIMBING

WHERE ARE YOU AT ON THE MOUNTAIN AND WHY ARE YOU STUCK THERE?

"Behold, I am doing a new thing; now it springs forth, do you not perceive it? I will make a way in the wilderness and rivers in the desert."

—Isaiah 43:19

-ESV-

"Starting Over"

I was divorced and started dating a guy that was one of my good friends when we were in high school. We used to laugh and say if we weren't married by the time we were 30 we would marry each other.

So that what we did. Even though we weren't quite 30 yet.

When we got married we also got his two children and I said God surely answered my prayers.

In 1998 We moved to Ohio for my husband's job and in September of that year I got really sick with Legionnaires Disease: my lungs were overflowing with blood and fluids and I was drowning.

I was on full life support and fell into a coma for nine months.

They called in my family because they said there was no life in me. No brain functions and they were going to take me off life support and let me die. In the middle of all the chaos when no one was looking, my children had put a huge Tweedy-Bird above my bed and my little boy whispered in my ear' "Mommy, if you can find the Tweedy-Bird you have found your way home.

Faith of a child!

My husband told the doctors no way would he allow them to take me off of life support! He told them they had no idea how much faith I had and wherever I was in this coma I was fighting to stay alive even if the machines and the hospital gadgets were saying something else. He made it clear they weren't going to touch me.

He stayed by my bed everyday making sure nothing would happen to me.

And one day I woke up.

The result: I had neurological brain damage because I had been without oxygen too long.

This meant I may never be able to function normally.

I would have to learn to read and write all over again. And the doctors were not real hopeful that I would ever fully regain those abilities.

Regardless of the results, three days later I went home. I did eventually learn to read and write again and that took about two years. It was during this time I started feeling like I needed to something more and I was tired of being home. I had worked since I was 13 and I was not one to sit around and do nothing so I decided to become a school teacher just because I knew I could overcome the challenge. And I did. I worked as a teacher for three years with kids who had behavior problems and abuse issues.

In 2001 I had five mini-strokes and ended

up almost dying. I was overweight at four hundred and thirty pounds on a five-foot two-inch body and my health. I was always having something wrong but I kept going anyway.

Going back to before I ended up in the coma, I had started putting on weight rapidly and would literally not eat all day.

It wasn't until I was almost dead they ran some tests and found out my thyroid was not working properly, and completely off the charts. I was so lethargic I couldn't even think.

They got me stabilized and put me on thyroid meds and a diet but I was already so heavy the diets didn't work that great and my health was suffering too. So, I stayed overweight even when I was in the coma.

After the mini-strokes, they did an emergency gastric bypass on me and I lost weight and was for the first time I was healthier and thinner than I had been in many years.

When I had reached my goal of 130 pounds it was then my husband told me he wanted a divorce that he had never loved me and that he was actually having an affair.

Once again, the happiness and love I spent my whole life looking for and thought I had, was all a big fat lie.

So, in 2003 I left.

[20] you should know that whoever turns a sinner from his wandering path will save him from death and cover many sins

James 5:20

-CJB-

"Wrong Way"

I started over but this time I went the opposite direction.

Forget God!

Forget Faith!

Forget this life!

I began going to the sports bars and then

the nightclubs meeting new people and making bad friends.

One night I got so messed up I couldn't drive. One of my "new friends" told me he had a pick me up and I snorted some cocaine and then hit a crack pipe.

Wow!

I was awake!!

And a few days later I was still awake.

I had lost three days of my life, work and well I didn't care. Every time my conscious tried to tell me I was wrong, I shoved it in a dark room and locked the door on it.

This was fun. I felt I could do anything.

But then the hour came when I was coming down, sweating, cramping, shaking. The worst feeling ever. So much so that I knew the only way to make it stop was to do more.

So, began my decline, everyday drinking and doping.

Remember it only took one bite of the apple to radically curse Adam and Eves life.

When your tuned out to the world and lost

in drugs time goes by quicker than you realize and you before too long your consumed.

This was me.

Before long I was smoking crack and ice and weed. I was taking "street" grade bars, pain killers and having huge pill parties like Russian Roulette never knowing what it is.

It was easier to stay high than to come down only to face the withdrawals and my misery.

Eventually I started dealing dope. It was a way to make mad money to pay for my high because I had a good job that paid the bills.

The Bible warns us of things like this all through the book of proverbs.

How our lusts will destroy us.

Wise in our own eyes.

The wicked woman... the folly... You name it it's in there.

And it's all true because my folly only led me further away from anything good and closer to death and hell.

It led me to the gang life.

I got accepted in the "bloods" and now, I couldn't share my life with my family anymore.

My daughter and son knew I was drinking and doping because they did it with me too. But they didn't know I was in a gang. I was truly living a double life. I was ashamed so I just kept trying to destroy my life.

Before long, I was getting chased by the cops, and been arrested a few times only to do a Houdini and escaped every time.

I had been run over by an SUV, thrown out of a truck on an overpass, gang raped by the Mexican mafia, hit by car again and had my face smashed into a cement culvert, and more cops.

My life had spiraled out of control.

I weighed 90 lbs.

I was broken beyond repair... I honestly felt that way.

I was getting sick, throwing up blood and having major pain when eating or drinking. My voice was raspy and sounded like I gravel rattling around every time I spoke. And I was still smoking cigarettes, about four packs a day, dipping Copenhagen and smoking cigars.

I had stopped eating except maybe a couple of crackers a day or an egg roll, because my life was consumed in a whiskey bottle along with all the other drugs. I would drink from the time I woke up until I passed out only to wake up and drink more.

Again, I knew I was sick and felt like I was dying and so I went to see my dad. He cried and insisted I see a doctor and he would pay for it. I did and the next thing I knew was sent to Baylor College of Medicine to a specialist.

I found out I had cancer again.

This time it was thyroid cancer and they wanted to start radical treatments.

I refused to have my throat cut and I refused to go through chemo or radiation. I had watched my aunt die going through that.

I told them forget it I'm dying anyway.

They said "you only have eight months if that

Jaimie."

I said "I guess you didn't hear me the first time, I am dying anyway, I'm a drug addict stupid and I don't care!"

My dad began to cry and begged me to let them take care of me.

I saw the desperation in his eyes and remorse of some kind to. But I was too far gone and I knew it.

So, I said "dad put me away somewhere, and throw away the key."

He said" NO, I could never do that, Jaimie!"

"No, you are my life. "

"I would rather die first."

He took me and made me eat that day, and I was so addicted I had the shakes.

He gave me some money knowing I was going to dope it and drink it. I guess he was more worried about my suffering, and didn't know anything about addictions. He thought he was helping me, he didn't realize he was hindering me from getting the help I really needed.

Eventually, my family turned away from me all

except my son and my dad.

My son kept trying to help me get away and go to church, but I said "NO"!

My dad did all he could do besides worry so he kept praying for me.

And he never stopped praying.

I sure am glad he didn't stop.

"In my distress I cried unto the LORD,
and he heard me. "

Psalm 120:1

–KJV–

"Distress Call"

One night I literally cried out to God, I was so angry and hurt I wanted to die.

I had tried to kill myself several times even drinking Clorox only to still be alive.

Why wouldn't God just let me go?

I was so full of hurt, anger and rage that I beat a hole in my kitchen floor screaming at God that night telling him "if you're real then show up!" It wasn't a cry it was a battle cry a charge for the Lord!

What happened next silenced me.

The very moment I demanded God to show up I saw the devil coming out of my wall. I wasn't high, What I saw was real and he told me I was his and that I wasn't ever going to talk to God or see him.

I was going to hell.

I cried harder than I had ever cried and I passed out.

The next morning my dad and step mom drove by my subdivision and my dad asked God to help me that he couldn't live without me. I was his miracle baby, He asked God to take him instead. My step-mom told him "forget it! it's too late, she is too far gone." But my dad had faith and began to cry and asked God with a desperate urgency "Please have her call me Please!"

By the time he got a block away his phone rang.

I was up after that rough night and I felt like I was going to die. I couldn't get the image of that demon out of my mind and I was really still angry with God for not even showing up. I had some of the gang hanging out with me and I even to this day don't know what it was, but I do know now whose voice it was that spoke inside me and said "call your dad and tell him you're ready to get help." "This is your last chance."

As soon as I heard that voice I told my friend" call my dad". He did and he talked to him and simply said "Jaimie wants you to come get her, she is ready to get help." And the moment he hung up the phone, I began convulsing and foam came out of my mouth and I hit the floor in a seizure.

My dad came and they loaded me in the back seat of my dad's car and they rushed me to the first hospital they could get to. I had such the reputation of disaster that the first hospital they took me too would not take me. They knew who I was and refused to help me. My dad drove another hour screaming through the city of Houston traffic and eventually found a hospital that would help me.

Saint Joseph's Hospital opened their door to me and after they detoxed me they were going to release me to the Police. I still didn't want to live. I was fighting so many demons in my life and they were trying to destroy me. And for what reason I don't understand even to this day, the nurse on duty handed me my big bag of prescription drugs. Fourteen bottles worth and well I took them all and flat lined right there.

A war had waged on my life between heaven and hell. And I spent another two weeks in the hospital.

Death...life...death...life!

I was under watch!!

I had police and Texas Marshalls outside my door and was going to go to prison after I was released.

But something supernatural happened instead.

I woke up to a tall African American man coming through my door with his Bible against his chest and when he walked in it was with the authority from heaven!!

Without speaking one word to me he pulled back the curtains and the sunlight shone through my window. As he approached the foot of my bed my body began to shake uncontrollably. He untied the straps from my ankles and broke the handcuffs on my wrists, he pulled the covers back and began to over my ninety pounds, beat up and broken-down body.

This mighty man of God...who was he?

He was speaking some language I had never heard before but I knew God was in my room.

He anointed me with oil from my head all the way to my toes and heels.

He began praying in English and in that other language and my body shook so hard I thought I was going to shake off the bed or explode.

He told me I would rise up from this bed and rise to my calling! He said it with such authority and the presence in my room was magnified so much I was consumed.

After he prayed he never said a word, he just left the room.

After he was gone I laid there crying and felt like I was five years old again.

I knew I had to go find God.

I crept out of my bed and the halls were empty and quiet enough to hear a pin drop.

I couldn't believe it.

No nurses, no cops...no patients... Where did everybody go??

Well I wasn't missing my chance. I took off and slid into the elevator and frantically began pushing the buttons in the elevator with no clue where I was going. But as the door opened and made the "ding" I saw a line of people and for I knew I was supposed to get in line.

I waited in line all the way until I got to the front and these preachers or priests put a little white thing in my mouth and gave me a little cup which I thought was wine. I ate the little cookie and drank the "grape juice" wine and they prayed over me and it felt so good even though I had absolutely no idea what it was I had just done. All I did know at that very moment is I wanted to do it again. So, I asked them how often they did this and they told me before lunch and before dinner.

Yes, I was there before lunch and then I showed up at dinner time too.

When they saw me before dinner time, they chuckled and asked me if I was saved, and I told them "I was alive yes and don't worry the cops don't know I'm here." and the one said "no are you saved, have you asked Jesus in your heart?"

That threw me completely off. Why did I need to ask Jesus into my heart?

So, I told them to explain this to me, tell me why I needed to ask Jesus into my heart.

When I found out about the plan of salvation I was so hurt and angry because no one had ever told me about this. And I had thought maybe God really didn't care about me anymore. I mean it seemed that way because since I was a child my life was a total wreck!

Now I am finding out my life has been a wreck because I never asked Jesus into my heart. I could have fixed my life a long time ago and all the church people including my dad held this information from me.

I was angry, but at the same time it was like someone giving me the key to real freedom.

I asked Jesus in my heart that day and to never let me go. I promised him I would try my very best to be what he wanted me to be for him.

That was the best day of my whole life.

It was also as if God started me right where

I had left off from when I was a kid in my heart again and I was a baby with his Word.

For the first time in my life I wanted to live.

The next day God performed another miracle. I was sentenced to seven years and was getting ready to be transported when God used the head nurse to make the call. She called the judge and fought for me and called a rehab and God opened a door for me to enter into a faith based Christian rehab, in Texas.

I knew God delivered me the day we drove up to the rehab because I got serious with him and told him if he wanted me to stay he would have to take the cravings for dope, cigarettes, alcohol and the lust away from me.

And He DID!

The moment I put my hand on the door to go inside God delivered me. It was as if He breathed a new air into my lungs. But I could smell the stench of my life on me still, but I knew I was free.

So far it seemed this walk with God was going great! Until I walked in there and found out I would be there for the next thirteen months.

No way was I going to stay that long!

The leaders and a few of the older students talked to me and showed me kindness that encouraged me.

I know I was being really immature about spending thirteen months of my life there but I was still so bound by the world that I didn't want to miss out on anything.

In thirteen months, people would forget about me too.

Then a young walked up to me and said "Jaimie it's only a season of life".

I finally agreed.

It wasn't easy.

The first night I woke up crying and all I wanted to do is to leave.

For the first time I was totally scared and unsure of what was happening to me.

I didn't have even the same boldness in me that I did at 13.

I felt cold, afraid and exposed and a prisoner all

in one.

I couldn't sleep I was having a panic attack but one of the intern's stayed with me all night and held me and prayed.

I'll never forget that lady and how kind she was to me.

J.L. Tipton

WRITE DOWN YOUR DISTRESS CALL TO GOD

"Wash yourselves clean!

Get your evil deeds out of my sight!
Stop doing evil,

17 learn to do good!
Seek justice, relieve the oppressed,
defend orphans, plead for the widow.

Isaiah 1:16-17

-CJB-

"Spiritual Boot Camp"

This faith-based rehab is spiritual boot camp. Many people think it's only for teenagers but it is for anyone with addictions of any kind. It's a tough place but it was the place God prepared for me. I know He knew how hard headed I was and what I needed to bring me to repentance and surrender.

I didn't like it and I didn't want to be there. My flesh crawled. At 4;30 am we were up bright and early our first duty as to make your bunk and it must be tight so that a quarter would bounce on it. I hated this part. And I failed at it every morning and would get written up during inspection. Three write ups and you get discipline that could be from 1 day to a month or longer. It was up to the women's director.

You had enough time to get dressed for the day and had to be in the chapel at 5:30 am for prayer. Every student is assigned a dorm leader (which is a student who has been there for a month or longer and possess the leadership skills to carry out the responsibility in a mature way.)

Mine was a beautiful teenage girl who knew she was beautiful and I didn't like her either. And she had to be glued to my side all day every day to show me what to do and how to do it.

Including praying out loud.

I didn't like this at all. I was a rebel in my heart. I was 39 years old and no teenager was going to give me orders.

One morning another young lady about 19 years old came up to me and scolded me because I was running late and told me she would write me up. I jumped up and kicked her knocking her down three flights of stairs and thankful I didn't kill her.

The next thing I knew I was being thrown to the ground and hog tied by the police. Before the were going to haul me off, the executive director a big muscle-built guy, got down on the ground and laid down and met me eye to eye and simply asked, "Jaimie, when are you going to live up to the potential God has for you?"

I could barely speak but I whispered in shame.

"I don't know how to".

He said "if I let you stay and don't press charges will you at least promise me you will try?"

I nodded my head yes and started to cry but fought the tears back.

I was sentenced to three months of word fast and a month was added to my program and I was on discipline.

Word fast is just that, you fast from talking period. No spoken word, no writing notes, no body language or else you earn an extra week for every time you break your word fast.

Discipline wasn't a slap on the hand or cleaning a toilet, no it was entirely different.

You were waking up several times throughout the night to move van seats. And sometimes given a big plastic spoon to scoop gravel and fill in holes.

Since I was the only one on discipline I had the job all to myself. The first wake up was at 11;30 pm I had five minutes to throw on some clothes and come downstairs, I was taken out back to see seven 15-passenger vans sitting out back of the chapel. The intern on duty was a tough one and she told me I would have to remove the van seats from all seven vans and drag them across the yard to the parsonage garage and stack them neatly.

Seriously?

I struggled with every one and wanted to beat this lady senseless. I completed it all and went back to bed never even taking my shoes off.

At 1:00 am I was being woke up again. I had to drag them all back and put them in the van.

This time she helped me load them and showed me how to put them in there. So, we were done in no time. I think she felt sorry for me.

At 3:00 am I was being woke up again to remove the seats and take them back to the parsonage.

At 4:30 we were waking up for dress and prayer and after prayer when everyone was going to breakfast I had to put the van seats back. Which meant breakfast would be cut short.

I did this for 3 months.

You would have thought I would be on my best behavior but I wasn't. My first morning after little to no sleep I griped to the cook about breakfast. So, I broke my word fast and I got another week added to word fast, another week of discipline all because I disrespected the cook. Protocol is you take your food and you thank them for it. No extras, no gripes and no questions.

I didn't care they weren't going to break me.

So, my added discipline was lost my first family visit.

What a struggle I felt in my soul.

After breakfast during the week we were sent to a factory next door that made and printed can cozies and t-shirts for many huge businesses including us.

We worked from 7 am until 4 pm every day. It wasn't an easy job, it was hot dirty and we only got two breaks. One for fifteen minutes and a thirty-minute lunch. After work we had to eat dinner and had five minutes shower time and ten minutes to get dressed and go to class until 8pm.

On Tuesday we had chapel night (church on campus) and Wednesday's we went to a church and from Thursday -Saturday some girls would work at the factory and the rest would go do fundraisers all day, standing outside big chain grocery stores and shopping marts selling crafts we made and asking people for a dollar.

I wasn't allowed to fundraise I was too gangster.

Which was true.

I looked rough and wasn't friendly.

The first time we went church on that Sunday, I got in trouble again.

When the preacher got up to preach I stood up and threw a song book at him and accused him of being a liar and a cheat and screamed several curse words at him also.

I really hated preachers and anyone religious.

When I was in my addiction, the church ladies would come to my house and be friendly and ask me to come to church. When I finally caved and went they began talking about me and the pastor looked at me like I was trash. After service I ran from there. And hated Christians even more.

I had seen many of the local preachers in the bars I went to and also caught one have sex with one of the school teachers.

Another one in city hall having sex with one of the district leaders and she was married too.

How could they get away with preaching when they lived a double standard?

They were hypocrites.

But the preacher that was bringing the Word that Sunday morning I had never met him, I just thought if one was dirty and all the ones I knew were dirty... well then, he must be dirty also.

I earned more word fast time and more discipline.

Sunday when everyone would come back to campus and get to rest, I had to work until it was time to go to evening service. I lost my phone call time with my family and I lost another visit. So, it was a month before I got to have my first family visit.

Family visits were every two weeks on a Sunday after church service and until 4pm. I thought I was really going to love seeing my mom and dad. And I was happy to see them until my step mom started criticizing me and reminding me how horrible I was and how I have worried my dad until he was physically sick and had lost forty-two pounds.

The last thing I needed to hear was what a horrible person I was and top it off with what a terrible daughter I am.

After that visit I was manically depressed again and it was as if literally all life had been sucked right out of me. I didn't want to read my bible and I didn't want to hear anything they had to say.

I just sunk deeper into the darkest place.

One day my teacher came to me and handed me a NIV Bible that was easier to read for me than KJV. I began trying to read but I was so depressed I just couldn't find any purpose to any of this. I thought wouldn't it had been better if they would have just locked me away in state facility and thrown away the key and just forgotten about me.

I couldn't come out of it either.

The women's director decided I needed to go through a deliverance program called "Committed to Freedom".

It is a study for anyone who has been through abuse physical and sexual. They prayed with me and I began the program.

I immediately hated it because it was pulling back parts of my life I buried and wanted to forget. Like an old bad tooth.

But once it is out there is relief and freedom, right?

I struggled sometimes just crying for hours.

They took me out of work and had me spend more time in class and in church services.

I was never allowed on the front row and never allowed to have any books with me in the chapel in fear I would throw them.

One evening we were at a church service and I laid down on the back pew.

I looked under the pew in front of me and well they forgot a songbook.

So, I slid it out from under the pew and I opened it up.

The song I opened it to pierced my heart so deep I began crying and couldn't stop.

For the first time in years, the tears flowed.

J.L. Tipton

"That I Could Still Go Free"

By: The Hinson's

Lock me up in a prison and throw away the key

Take away the vision, from these eyes that now, now I see

Then deprive me of the food I eat, and even bind my hands and feet

For as long as I know Jesus, I can still go free.

That I could go free

what kind of man would reach down his hand and do this for me?

Unworthy to live and not fit to kill

Yet a man on a cross, Put me in His will

And said I could still go free.

Now I could never quite understand

Why a King would wanna leave His throne

Put on the robe of and earthly man

And feel the pain of flesh, flesh and bone

Then to later trod that lonely path, that led to Calvary.

But those blood red stains, broke all my chains

So that I could still Go Free.

Now, "ADONAI" in this text means the Spirit. And where the Spirit of ADONAI is, there is freedom.

2 Corinthians 3:17

-CJB-

"Breaking Chains"

From that moment on It was almost like there was no more gangster girl left in me, God was knocking on my heart and for the first time in years I remember I cried... and cried!!

These words....

there is this man called Jesus...

I met him in the hospital...

He really did have my back.

All this time I have treated him so badly...

yet... He loved me anyway!

Reading and thinking about the only one who loved me more than life itself, made me realize how weak I was and how much I needed Him.

Everyone was staring at me and in shock that I was crying. Snot slinging crying and I couldn't stop.

And then I opened my mouth, "quit looking at me or I will kill you all!"

Yeah right!

That night I hugged that book so tight and asked my director if I could have it. Of course, it belonged to the church we were visiting and the Pastors wife was kind and took the book and made a copy of the song for me. She also wrote a prayer of hope on the copy for me.

I took that song and hung it by my bunk bed and read it every night before I went to sleep along with the prayer she had written out for me.

God started changing my heart.

I was doing great and I made peace with where I was. But that was just a small frame of time because it wasn't long at all before the devil came back and tried me again.

This time I got mad at the intern in charge of me because she lied to me and about me and wrote me up. So, when she brought the write up for me to sign I took the pen and tried to stab her in the hand, instead I purposely missed by a half inch and stabbed the table so hard the pen stuck in the wood.

I ran out of the building, scaled the ten-foot fence and left the program. I headed to the nearest phone and called my old boyfriend and my dad.

While I waited to see who would show up a lady in the store came and bought me a coffee and talked to me and told me her story about how she used to be an alcoholic and how she lost her children and how God gave her another chance. She prayed with me and I listened to everything she said. I didn't really want to leave the program but I didn't want everyone telling me lies either.

Well that's what I told myself anyway.

The truth was I didn't want to let go of my control over my life.

If I couldn't be submissive to authority of man then how could I ever learn to be submissive to Gods authority.

After hours of waiting, my dad is the one who showed up.

He talked me into going back and I knew they wouldn't take me and I would end up going to prison.

But even knowing all that I went back anyway and promised I wouldn't leave or cause any more trouble again, that I was ready to get serious about my life.

They let me stay.

I cry today when I think about how God intervened in my mess and gave me favor.

I was going on six months and was still getting in some trouble but I was trying to do better and when I was disciplined I was accepting of it and understood. I was learning to submit.

I was still dealing with great amounts of depression and I was on the halfway point of my committed to freedom program.

The part where you start giving names to the bricks you have used to build a wall in your life that keeps everyone out including God.

These were my strongholds keeping me feeling

like I was protected from...

I had a lot of bricks and a lot of different names I called them.

It was paralyzing me. I knew it was much bigger than me.

And in the middle of the biggest storm we had in years in Texas God began my deliverance.

Therefore, confess your sins to one another [your false steps, your offenses], and pray for one another, that you may be healed and restored. The heartfelt and persistent prayer of a righteous man (believer) can accomplish much [when put into action and made effective by God—it is dynamic and can have tremendous power].

James 5:16

-KJV-

"Deliverance"

We were being evacuated to San Antonio, Texas to get safely away form the hurricane that was coming in. Along the way I began getting deathly ill in the van, and I was the driver. They pulled over and I got in one of the bench seats and laid down.

Along the trip the ladies in the van all started screaming because I was being choked and they saw a demon on me choking me.

Everyone saw it and they pulled the van off the highway. All the other vans following us pulled over too and the pastors got out and came and prayed over me.

I began throwing up uncontrollably. After things settled down we got back on the road. Several hours later we pulled over again for the same reason. By this time no one wanted to be in the van with me, but the pastors and their wives did and they stayed with me all the way to San Antonio.

When we arrived, it was dark. We pulled up and when inside the multi-purpose building to see over 300 cots and there were 300 of us there to fill them. The minute I walked in they were singing praises to God and I immediately came under attack again and this time having seizures.

I was running a high fever and they decided they would call 911. But I said "NO!" "Please just pray over me."

Have you ever heard three hundred people pray out loud at the same time? It was the most beautiful thing I had ever heard in my life and it was healing.

A couple more times that evening the demons were attacking me and yet the people laid hands all together over me and prayed. Each time I felt peace and healing.

Then at 2 am I woke up knowing I was going to throw up. So, I crawled on my hands and knees to the ladies' room. I had to crawl because I was too weak to stand. As I hugged the toilet I began to cry and asked God "why?" And then it finally came out of my mouth, "Lord, please...please...please forgive me."

I crawled out of the bathroom and I heard God speak to me and He said "come meet me here." I knew the third pew back was where I was to go and there I began to pray and ask God to forgive me of all the sins I could remember and even the ones I couldn't remember.

I prayed and got repented and to be sure I was saved I asked Jesus into my heart and then I said to God, "I give you my life, all of it, I surrender my life, heart, my soul and my will to yours Lord from this moment on." When I said "Amen" I lifted my head to see it was 11:30 am the next day. I had been on prayer all that time.

Oh, and wait a minute...

AND LET ME TELL YOU...

I was new!

I felt brand new!

God delivered me from devils and demons and healed me.

Seizures-HEALED

Asthma-HEALED

Thyroid Cancer- HEALED

Bi-Polar Disease- HEALED

Depression- HEALED

I surrendered my life to Him that day and He delivered me.

From that day on I grew in truth and spirit and I fell completely in love with God. I danced with him in the rain, I looked for him in the clouds, and he called me friend!!

**WRITE DOWN WHAT YOU HAVE OR WANT TO
BE HEALED OF AND DELIVERED FROM**

WRITE DOWN HOW GOD HAS HEALED YOU

4 Through immersion into his death we were buried with him; so that just as, through the glory of the Father, the Messiah was raised from the dead, likewise we too might live a new life.

Romans 6:4

–CJB–

J.L. Tipton

"Ice Water Baptism"

One day we went to a church in Houston
Texas and the pastor was preaching about
Esther. The one thing that strummed the
chords of my heart is when the preacher said it
wasn't about Esther, it was about what God
wanted for Esther because it was to save a
people. I thought about the people who were
still out there in this world that were truly lost.
God created them but they didn't know Him.
I wanted what God wanted for me too.

So, when the altar call was made I ran to it and I didn't just get filled with the Holy Spirit I got Baptized with in the Holy Spirit. I began speaking in tongues and stayed consumed for hours. God gave me Ezekiel 3 and I read it over and over, but I didn't understand what God was trying to tell me.

That was for another time.

After that day, I got baptized.

That was another move of God in my life.

After I surrendered and everyone knew it was real, they wanted me to get baptized. But I

constantly told them "Only when God tells me to, will I get baptized."

One winter morning we went to give testimony in Angleton, Texas at a Cowboy Church. When we got there, we saw the church was being held under a big tent, outside. As I was sitting there I felt the Holy Spirit tell me "today is the day you will get baptized."

I thought, "okay who is going to tell the preacher?"

As the preacher opened his mouth he said "God says someone is getting baptized today."

I jumped up and shouted "It's Me!"

Pastor Reg giggled and asked me if I came with clothes and immediately a lady jumped up and said "I have clothes for her, God told me

 someone would need them today and to put them in the trunk of my car!"

There was so much excitement from just what God was doing. I had never even met these people before until that day.

Before I got changed the preacher said "well we only have one problem." "we only have a horse trough to baptize you in and since its only 27 degrees outside its frozen." I said "well pastor can we break the ice?" He said "yes I imagine we can."

I said "Awesome, lets get me in that water then!"

I never felt the water.

I couldn't tell you if it was freezing or boiling.

I only know it was God ordained and when I went down in the water I came up speaking in tongues and the light of God was all over me!

 I will always remember that day too!

The next weekend I was in the middle of nowhere at a gas station fundraising and a bus was rounding the curve where the little gas station sat. It came to a screeching halt and a young man about 18 jumped off the bus and ran straight to me and said "I want to be saved."

I had never led anyone to the Lord before and I was so scared but I wasn't going to let my fear hold me back from what God had appointed me that day. So, I led him to the Lord and he called his family to tell them he had given his heart to the Lord.

I was still in shock and shaking and called Pastor Reg and told him what happened. He cried and told me how he had been praying that God would use me to lead someone to the Lord. That I wouldn't be stagnant ever in my walk.

From there the fire in my soul to serve God and be used by Him grew even more.

Time flew by and before I knew it I was graduating. I couldn't believe the time really was just a short season that I had been there.

They asked me if I would stay on as a staff member and work in the finance department.

I was amazed how God transformed my life going from a person no one trusted to being called a woman of integrity.

I kept working for them learning and growing in every part of the ministry that God was leading me in.

Therefore I, the prisoner united with the Lord, beg you to lead a life worthy of the calling to which you have been called.

Ephesians 4:1

-CBJ-

"The Call"

One day driving to cash my first paycheck I was praying and beckoning God what my call was, where would I go from here. As I prayed I came upon an intersection off the freeway and looked over to my left. There under the freeway were at least a hundred homeless including crippled and little children.

I was devastated to see this especially the heat outside was 112 degrees in the shade.

I immediately saw fast food hamburger joint to my right and drove up to it and went inside.

When I got up to the counter I remembered the only money I had on me was my first paycheck. So, I asked her how many hamburgers fries and drinks could I buy with it as I slid it across the counter.

She went and got the manager.

So, I asked him the same question and told him why I needed to know.

Well God was in that whole appointment, because he not only let me use my check and just sign it over but the manager matched my check and him and his employees helped carry food under the freeway to all the people.

The move of God was touching customers too because before I knew what was happening people were buying food and drinks and bringing it to the people. So many times, we think one-person can't change anything. But that is dead wrong. One person can change the whole outcome.

From that day forward God had me helping the homeless. It was wonderful and even the rehab allowed me once a week to take a group of ladies out to feed and minister in the alleys of the worst parts of Houston, Texas.

It wasn't long after that God started speaking to me that it was time to move on to the next part of the plan He has called me to.

In the meantime, I did all the schooling I needed and received my certifications in Biblical Counseling and Personal Studies for New Christians which allowed me to teach the curriculum that was used. I learned the accounting department and I began speaking in the churches. These are just a few of the things I never imagined I would do in my life.

Never underestimate the power of God in your life. It is when you realize and become reverent to the fact that without God we are nothing. It is only because of Him and with Him we are given power and strength and abilities to do the things we could never do on our own.

The day had come that God spoke to me and told me He was moving me to Missouri to give me a ministry and a husband.

I wrestled with God on this only because I was afraid one of leaving my family and two because I didn't want a husband. I had been through marriages and they all ended badly and I sure didn't want to risk marrying another cheater or abuser.

So, for three months I dealt with troubles because I wouldn't leave when I was supposed to.

One day I got a crazy phone call. On the other end of the line was a man I had ministered to a lot because he was addicted to crack.

When he spoke I knew who it was but how did he get my cell number? This number wasn't even in my name it was in my dad's name. So, I asked him. And he began to speak stuttering so bad you could hardly understand him.

"Jaimie, Jaimie," he stuttered, "God came to me and woke me up last night and Jaimie He gave me your number."

I said "you are lying."

he said "No Jaimie, I wouldn't lie to you." "Jaimie, God told me to tell you to quit arguing with him, He said He is sending you to Missouri to give you a ministry on a hill and a husband and you are happy Jaimie."

I was paralyzed with a fear I had never felt before.

I knew God had my ticket and I was in trouble. I promised the guy I would obey God and go to Missouri.

So how was this going to take place. I didn't know anyone in Missouri.

No matter how it was all supposed to happen I told God I would go wherever He sent me. And I got repented for wrestling with Him.

I went and packed up my things and waited to see what would come next. And two weeks later the president of the rehab came to see me and said I had been personally requested by another rehab in Arkansas and would I consider it. I told them I would go.

They prayed a blessing over me and I left the next day.

The day I left was also the day my real mom was in the hospital and dying. They had called in all of us to come say our goodbyes. I called her on the phone and said I couldn't stop to see her that God would heal her. She was dying and yet managed to tell me: what kind of God would not let you come see me? Don't ever call me again!" and slammed the phone down.

I cried and asked God "WHY?"

He spoke to me and said "your obedience to me will bring healing to your mom, just keep moving and I will save her."

So, I praised Him and kept on driving.

I drove to Russellville, Arkansas and oddly the Lord told me not to unpack and unpack only what I would need. So, I stored all my boxes in the garage and only kept the basics out. I had no clue how Arkansas was the Missouri path but God knew.

After about nine months passed, I got a call one day from the vice president of the Arkansas rehab campus asking me to come to the main office for a meeting. I was a little nervous and well I had no idea what to expect.

When I walked in he looked me in the eyes with a huge smiled and said "Sister Jaimie, how about Missouri?"

I looked at him and without hesitation I blurted out "I'll Go!"

He laughed and said "well you don't even know what I am going to ask you."

"Oh yes sir, I do know because God already told me where I am going, so yes I will go."

"Jaimie, your too spiritual'"

He told me that and I remember thinking, how can anyone be too spiritual.

I'm just in love with God.

Isn't everyone supposed to have a relationship with Him like this?

That week they prepared me for my duties at the new center they had opened in Springfield, Missouri.

By the end of the week I was on my way.

for never has a prophecy come as a result of human willing — on the contrary, people moved by the Ruach HaKodesh spoke a message from God.

2 Peter 1:21

-CJB-

"Confirmation"

I am going to take to back for a minute to a time before I came to Missouri. A time God was confirming the things that He had spoken to me years before.

"I am moving you to Missouri to give you a ministry and a husband."

When God spoke that to me I had no idea It wouldn't be immediate. But Gods time is not our time. It just proves we have conditioned ourselves to live in an instant world. I want it now. I mean you can go through a drive through and get a meal to feed the family in less than five minutes. That doesn't mean what is instant or quick is good for you.

God is patient and He only works in a perfect will and in perfect time.

I had moved to Arkansas, and well I honestly couldn't see how God was using Arkansas to bring me to Missouri.

He used the Arkansas ministry and everything about it to fulfill His perfect will in my life and He did it in a way that appeared to be a mess up.

One day we were getting ready for all the weekend fundraisers and I was really looking forward to this weekend in particular because I was getting to fundraise at a huge store that the people not only donated a lot but loved the ministry. Just when I had all my stuff ready, the Women's Director came to me and told me they were changing my store. I was upset.

She told me that a new lady was coming in that night who was a heroin addict and she needed me to oversee her and help her, so they would send me to a small store in Pocahontas, Arkansas.

I was upset about not getting to go to the big

store, but after I surrendered my life to God I viewed every appointment a "divine appointment" for God.

So, I without hesitation told her I would do it.

When we got to the store the next day, the lady was struggling so bad. She hadn't even been detoxed yet and she was coming down off of heroin hard. I felt so sorry for her and I felt helpless.

On top of her struggling, no one was nice to us. I even had some devil worshippers spit on me.

Every hour we were required to a do a count of money that each lady had collected in donations and by selling crafts and I had to call it in to the rehab main office. (accountability).

This meant I had to leave this lady alone at the one side of the store (outside) while I did the count with the ladies at the other end. I was so scared to leave her because God was telling me she was going to run.

So, I prayed for her before I walked away.

While I was at the other end collecting the lady's money and writing it all down, I hear a loud cry come from the other end of the store and in terror I turned around to see what was going on.

Here was a big tall man laying hands on this lady who was coming down and she had her arms in the air crying out to God and was speaking in tongues. This man had his hand on her head and was praying over her and y first thought especially when I realized there were about fifty people standing around him and her... "Oh, no this cant happen out here, they will come tell us we have to leave and I will get fired!"

I began my walk to the other side to stop this and I felt a hand on me and voice that said "don't touch mine anointed."

It humbled me and I knew I wasn't supposed to say or do anything but at the moment I was so scared of being in trouble with the store and the rehab that I went anyway.

When I got down there the spirit of God was so heavy I couldn't speak and all I could do is put my hand on the arm of the man praying and join in.

He said," Amen" and looked down at me and the first thing I noticed was his beautiful blue eyes. Not in a way that your thinking. It was a Godly thing, they were the bluest eyes I had ever seen.

He smiled at me and said "WELL PRAISE THE
LORD SISTER!" (street preachers are loud)

I said, "Praise the Lord, what's your name?" (I
needed it to explain who this man was if I had
gotten in trouble)

He responded with "WELL, THEY CALL ME
THE CRAZY PREACHER!"

I wanted to drop everything and just run back
to Texas. I was going to get fired for sure when
I have to tell them "Oh, it's okay because the
"Crazy Preacher" prayed for her"."

Instead I got mad stomped my foot at him and
said "WHAT IS YOUR GOD GIVEN NAME?"

He looked a bit scared. And said very softly
"well that would be Tim Tipton, ma'am."

I said with frustration, "THANK YOU!"

And I walked away. I don't know why I walked
away but I think it was I was at that moment
more afraid God was mad at me.

When I got to the other side, the ladies were
filled with the Holy Spirt and were crying and
praising God and I just gave in and thought I

don't want to mess up what God is doing. I set my clipboard on the craft table and stood there for a moment and one lady stopped speaking in tongues and said "Ms. Jaimie, God said that man down there is going to be your husband."

I looked at her and without saying anything, laughed.

I thought in my mind, "lady, you have no clue what your talking about, God said my husband is in Missouri, this guy is in Arkansas."

When the "Crazy Preacher" came out of the store he came out and got in a bus loaded with a bunch of guys. He drove down to my end where I was praying for one of the young men that were waiting to get on that bus. When they pulled up the side of the bus read POWER OF FREEDOM MINISTRIES.

I felt horrible about stomping my foot at the preacher and being so mean. I stepped up on the bus and apologized and hugged the preacher. He gave me his testimony and it had a number and email address on it if you need prayer day or night.

I immediately felt God tug my heart to encourage these guys also by telling them stay where God had them. I realized they were a men's rehab and I wanted to encourage them to stay for the long haul.

I thanked them all and the preacher too for praying for the lady because she was a new woman that prayer changed her life!

They drove away and I never gave it a second thought.

The time came that I had to take the lady who got delivered that day to court for her custody trial for her twin boys. I decided to email that "Crazy Preacher" who had prayed for her and asked that he pray for her situation and for me to have the right words to speak.

I know he did because the favor of God was all over her court situation. The judge ruled in her favor and she got full custody of her children. I knew this may cause her to leave the program early but when we got to the car she said "I am not leaving until God tells me to, I want what you have with God."

Her family took care of her children while God worked mightily in her life and she graduated and went to work there.

I would text the phone number for the "Crazy Preacher" and just share testimony of how that prayer changed her life and mine too.

We became prayer friends but never spoke in person or over the phone, just strictly prayer and I would say if you're in this area can you go by and encourage the ladies who are fundraising.

He always would too.

The years passed and a another one was almost gone and by this time I was in Missouri heling run the women's center there.

One day he had texted me about a young man and his children who we had prayed would give their hearts to the Lord. I knew the ladies where too busy struggling in their own mess and thought if I give them a family to pray for fervently that they would come out of their woes and let God heal them by being and instrument for him. When I told them the story of this family they broke and before I could ask they said "Ms. Jaimie can we pray for them?"

They prayed everyday for this single father and his five children out loud taking turns lifting each child's name up to God with a specific request for them. This went on for almost a year. Even the new ladies that were coming in to the rehab were taking on these fervent prayers for this family.

One night about 2 am I came in from driving us back from a fundraiser and was exhausted. I saw a text on my phone that said "PRAISE THE LORD! THEY GAVE THEIR HEARTS to GOD AND I JUST BAPTIZED the DAD AND ALL FIVE CHILDREN!"

It was from the Crazy Preacher.

I was so blown away, I texted him back saying "you mean you just now baptized them at 2 am?"

He texted. "YES" and then asked me "what are you doing up so late?" So, I told him I had just got in from a fundraiser.

He asked me if he could call me and share what happened and I needed to be encouraged and I couldn't wait to be able to know the whole story to tell the ladies so I said "YES!"

As we talked he told me about how they had been having revival in this little town of Ellington and how they had been preaching all day and baptizing.

I was so jealous!

I had never been to anything like this and I

wanted to see this kind of the move of God in whatever ministry God was calling me to.

He told me how this move of God also happened with the homeless and I was just so excited for them and for my journey too. It was as if God was reminding me what He called me to and the in between time I am in the journey that to not be discouraged.

Because I was.

I was so consumed in the testimony I no longer felt tired. I realized though this man had to be tired and had a long drive ahead of him because he said he was going home.

I said "well I know you have a long, long drive." He giggled a bit and said "well I am preaching and baptizing again tomorrow here too."

I said "so you're going to drive all the ay home and all the way back?"

He giggled again and said "well sure, why not."

I said "Well bless you to have to do that and drive that far."

He laughs and said, "It's not far at all only 2 miles outside of town."

I said, "but you're in Missouri right now."

He said, "You know I thought that too" and laughed and said "where do you think I live?"

I said, "Arkansas?" questioning now in my mind everything.

He laughed and said "Sister, I live right here in Missouri. I have 31 acres of land outside of town on a hill and a Women's ministry, just no one to help me run it."

I hung up on him and began fasting and praying for twelve days.

I never told him what God had spoke to me.

I wanted God to speak to him.

When I spoke to him again he asked me why I hadn't been answering texts, email or phone calls from him and I said well I was fasting and praying. He said "me too"

Then he called for Moses and Aaron at night and said, "Get up, get out from among my people, both you and the Israelites; and go, serve the LORD, as you said.

Exodus 12:31

-AMP-

"Called Out"

Another year was passing, and we were becoming closer friends and prayer partners. The ladies would come back from fundraisers and be all excited that the "Crazy Preacher" had come by and prayed for them and encouraged them. He would send us DVDs of the street ministry he did with the homeless and in the crack houses and it would show them getting delivered. The women were really grabbing ahold of a relationship with God through that.

I did also ad I remember, God showing me how

I needed to take my spare time and go feed the homeless also. So, I did, I began volunteering at a shelter to help feed the people coming in and I got to pray for them to and minister in their lives. It was amazing!

As another year flew by, I heard God speak to me to prepare me my time here with the rehab was ending. I began preparing myself through obedience and prayer each day what God wanted me to do.

The day came and God told me "honor your pastors and leaders and give them a notice on April 8th I am taking out of here to move you to the ministry I have called you to only this time my daughter they will not bless you, instead they will curse you and doubt my presence in you, be obedient and leave a good name for yourself, I am with you and I will bless you where man cannot."

This excited me and terrified me. They were going to curse me.

BUT I HAD GOD ON MY SIDE!

The next morning, I wrote out the letter to my leaders exactly as God instructed me to do. At first, they were honored and then the next morning they gave me a letter also that read:

"YOU HAVE 72 HOURS TO REMOVE YOUR
PERSON AND PROPERTY FROM HERE OR WE
WIL HAVE YOU ESCORTED BY THE SHERIFF,
DO NOT SPEAK TO ANY OF THE LADIES
STUDENTS OR LEADERS. YOU ARE ON A
CORPORATE WORD FAST AND IF YOU BREAK
IT AT ANYTIME IN THE 72 HOURS YOU WILL
BE IMEDIATELY REMOVED FROM THE
PREMISES.

WE ALSO DO NOT BELIEVE GOD HAS SPOKEN
THIS TO YOU AND WILL NOT GIVE YOU OUR
BLESSING."

My first thought was "UGH! And they call
themselves Christians."

I began to shake, but not cry. I went to my
room and I prayed and I told my Daddy in
heaven on them. I showed Him the letter they
gave me. But God didn't jump out of heaven
and defend me. Instead my phone rang.

It was the "Crazy Preacher".

I didn't know what to say to him when he
called. But I knew I needed to let him know
what was going on.

A few times in the past we talked about if it
was Gods will that if I came to Ellington, I

could help run his Free Store called; HEAVENS CLOSET. It was a store that had everything from clothing to furniture to toys and appliances. I asked him one day "If it is HEAVENS CLOSET then why do you call it the FREE STORE?" He said," Because everything in it is free...just like in heaven, its free because Jesus died for us and in Heavens Closet everything is free because God gave it."

I loved the whole idea. But still how was I going to explain what was going on this day.

I got quiet and he said, "I been praying for you today and I felt God telling me to call and pray with you and for you." I immediately broke into tears and told him what was going on.

He encouraged me and told me not to worry he would send a friend with a trailer and would pick me up and haul my car and I could live in the FREE STORE.

He also informed me there's no paycheck here in this ministry. If you come it is by faith and you will live on faith, ministry is fulltime.

Before I could talk myself out of it, I said "YES."

The next day he showed up with a friend and

we loaded all my belongings including my car on the trailer and we left Springfield and headed to what would be my new home.

WAIT!

You mean I am going to live in the back of a business... I am officially homeless. I am so ill-equipped for this... my family is going to think I am crazy or on drugs again... Who does this?

WAIT!

I am allowing a "preacher" but a stranger to me to help me. And I am moving farther away from my family. What if I get there and something happens?

Oh, I had to tell my mind to shut up and I said goodbye to all the ladies and they circled around me and prayed with me.

Except for some wild imagination's I actually had a great peace covering me.

Before I had also worried a little how God would supply things I needed especially personal needs. But God had everything I would need waiting there for me.

I never had a need or a want that God didn't use people to come and help me with and they had no idea it was God using them for that reason.

The first week I was at the FREE STORE, the preacher handed me the key, told me how everything went and told me I it a priority to ask people if they need prayer. He said, "I am going to St. Louis to feed, minister and camp out with the homeless for two weeks, you're in charge." And he left.

My first week I was a little nervous...okay inside I didn't know if I was overly nervous or overly excited because here I was stepping into the place God positioned me to be in but only for a season.
I LOVED THIS LIFE!!!

Seasons in our life change and with each new season being different from the last. My season began to change drastically just in the first month I was here. I had seen so many struggling people. Some would come in for prayer in the early morning and seem to be great after we prayed. And then about 2pm in the afternoon I would see them walking through town, staggering and had urinated on themselves and were totally unaware of it or anyone. It was gravely sad and almost unbearable for me to watch. Why didn't they let

God be concrete in their life? I watched them get delivered...

Then God reminded me of scripture...

The thing spoken of in the true proverb has happened to them, "The dog returns to his own vomit," and, "A sow is washed only to wallow [again] in the mire."

2 Peter 2:22 -AMP-

Then one day I was really discouraged because all the ministry that was being poured out and no one was really grabbing ahold. They wanted delivered in the morning and by afternoon they were bound again. So, I was so down I stared out the FREE STORE window asking God if I in fact did something wrong and that is why I was sent here.

About the time I was in a pity party an eight-year-old girl became frantically beating on the door crying and screaming for help!

The little girl came home to find her mom dead. The paramedics and police had come the neighbors were there and the dead woman's mom was there. And this little girl told me "You just have to come with me, you know Jesus and it has to be you to pray and bring my mommy back!" "PLEASE..." I let her lead the way holding my hand and we ran over to her house. When I walked in the room the lady was laying in her bed blue and cold and swollen with a Fentanyl patch stuck to her tongue.

The paramedics told me its too late we have tried everything she is gone.

I went into the living room and saw this little girl standing there looking into my soul for hope.

She was looking for Jesus.

And she knew I knew Him.

Now how would Jesus fix this?

I told the family to come into the living room and we all got down on the floor holding hands and began praying in belief that God would resurrect this little girl's mommy from the dead.

While we were in the middle of the prayer I stopped and looked at the paramedics and said "hit her again." something and before he could I said "GOD SAYS GO BACK IN THERE AND DO IT AGAIN NOW!"

He ran into the room and I heard a moan and then a cry from the paramedic hollering for help.

That evening we went to see her in the ICU and she was sentenced to prison. But her request was that we help her little girl and watch over her until a family member could get custody for her.

I couldn't have been happier to help and the bonus was I had a little friend in the FREE STORE with me.

I want to pause and reflect a moment how in my time of discouragement and wondering if God was mad at me how He showed up that instant to get me busy about His business.

I needed that so very much.

He has made everything beautiful in its time. He also has planted eternity in men's hearts and minds [a divinely implanted sense of a purpose working through the ages which nothing under the sun but God alone can satisfy], yet so that men cannot find out what God has done from the beginning to the end.

ECCLESIASTES 3:11

-AMPC-

"Gods' Time"

As the weeks passed we were asked to come and help with the church camp program and I was so excited about helping since I never had an opportunity to be in a church camp growing up due to being in a religion that didn't allow that. So was another season was budding an it was a time that would speed up. We went to the camp and Crazy Preacher was asked to minister to the teenagers about dating. It was then he was explaining to them that it is dangerous to date to see if you like someone, because it can lead to exploring areas of life that God holds sacred for marriage only. He told them how when you court you do so with the intent to marry that person. At that moment he paused and turned to me asked "Sister Jaimie I would love to court you to marry you someday soon." "Will you go out with me, not to date but to marry?"

At that moment the whole class stood up and cheered saying "ITS ABOUT TIME!"

Maybe to them it was about time he asked me but to me it was Gods perfect time because I never spoke a word or even gave an idea that we were anymore than friends and ministry together. Especially to him.

I wanted it to be ALL GOD.

Blushing I said "yes I would love to be courted by you."

We dated for almost six months and God spoke to him in the middle of a revival. He was preaching and, in the middle of preaching, he stopped and dropped to his knees and asked me to marry him on August 19th. I said "Yes!" with great joy.

He told me that day, "I am sorry I don't have a ring to give you."

I told him "I'm not worried, God will bring it."

I wanted my Abba Father to tell me what pleased Him. What dress I would wear, if I was supposed to even have a ring, I wanted Him to pick it. I didn't want us interfering with Gods plan even to the smallest details.

A month before our wedding God brought me a dress. He sent a lady I didn't know to bring it and say "God told me to give this to you."

Then two weeks before the wedding Crazy Preacher was in the grocery store and the cashier asked him "are you getting married soon or something?" He said, "yes I am, in two weeks as a matter a fact." At that moment the cashier dropped a ring into his hand with his change and said "Well God said you're going to need this."

He started to laugh and cry because only God can do these things.

He showed me the ring and told me what happened and he wanted to make sure it fit. So, I tried it on and it was too small.

We preached at a church the following Sunday

and received an $80.00 love offering. He took me and my ring to the jewelers and they told us it would cost $80.00 to size it bigger.

Imagine that!

The lady asked me how we came by the ring and I told her how God worked everything out. She stood in disbelief and glared at me and said "Why would God do that for you?" I said because like you are, I too am His princess. He cares about the smallest and the biggest details of my life. He is the one who holds my past my present and my future in His hands. Why wouldn't He do it for me?"

We left the ring and as we left, I told Tim that "I think that lady might have thought we stole that ring. I bet she does a history on it". and giggled because I knew God would prove the truth to her.

A week past and we were heading to the store to get some finishing things for our wedding day. (Candy for the homeless) and the lady for the jewelry store saw me and literally ran to me. She was in her seventies and running to me.

As she got up to me she was already crying and grabbed me caught her breath and begged me to come to the jewelry store.

I laughed because I thought "I bet the ring is stolen." And then I told God I was sorry for thinking that.

As we got in the store she told me she did the history on the ring and had it appraised.

She began to cry and shake and handed me the ring and it was glistening and spoke through her tears saying," this ring is a princess cut diamond ring. It is a past, present and future ring." And she began to cry again.

I reached around and hugged her and told her we are Gods princesses. She looked up at me and said "I want what you have." "I am seventy-two years old, I have been in church my whole life and I have never really been saved."

So, I led her to the Lord that day right there in the jewelry store.

Maybe the ring God brought me was just for her. It was God used to show her how important to Him she was and at seventy-two she could still be His princess.

Every year I would go back and see her and bring her a gift that god would have me get for her. Something so personal only she and God knew about what it meant to her.

In 2016 I went to see her and found she had passed away.

I know she is in Heaven.

Everything God did to lead us up to this time was prophetic...

Confirmed and...

Fulfilled.

The next step was heading to St. Louis to get married with the homeless.

On August 19th 2010 we got married at the homeless camp in St. Louis Missouri. So many people came to celebrate and  help make that day happen.

Misfits for Jesus came and supplied all the food and drinks and sound equipment, chairs clothing for the homeless and love.

Our great friend and fellow street preacher married us and We even had the homeless in our wedding party.

And people who call us "family" came to celebrate this day with us.

Since that day and today we have been living life to the fullest, still living completely on faith.

Together we love serving God and thanking God for Salvation...

leading others to know who Jesus is.

For if you fail to speak up now, relief and deliverance will come to the Jews from a different direction; but you and your father's family will perish. Who knows whether you didn't come into your royal position precisely for such a time as this."

Esther 4:14

-CJB-

"For Such a Time as, This"

I am thankful that since I have gotten saved I have learned to know now what true love is.

It is first the love we find in our Lord and Savior and in God above.

Real true love is never found in people and things.

That is a lie of the devil to keep you discouraged.

You see I realize now whether or not anyone in my life ever really loved me has nothing to do with why I was born.

I was born for God because psalm 139:1–18 (CJB) says;

I Adonai, you have probed me, and you know me.

2 You know when I sit and when I stand up,

you discern my inclinations from afar,

3 you scrutinize my daily activities.

You are so familiar with all my ways

4 that before I speak even a word, Adonai,

you know all about it already.

5 You have hemmed me in both behind and in front

and laid your hand on me.

6 Such wonderful knowledge is beyond me,

far too high for me to reach.

7 Where can I go to escape your Spirit?

Where can I flee from your presence?

8 If I climb up to heaven, you are there;

if I lie down in Sh'ol, you are there.

J.L. Tipton

9 If I fly away with the wings of the dawn

and land beyond the sea,

10 even there your hand would lead me,

your right hand would hold me fast.

11 If I say, "Let darkness surround me,

let the light around me be night,"

12 even darkness like this

is not too dark for you;

rather, night is as clear as day,

darkness and light are the same.

13 For you fashioned my inmost being,

you knit me together in my mother's womb.

14 I thank you because I am awesomely made,

wonderfully; your works are wonders —

I know this very well.

15 My bones were not hidden from you

when I was being made in secret,

intricately woven in the depths of the earth.

16 Your eyes could see me as an embryo,

but in your book all my days were already written;

my days had been shaped

before any of them existed.

17 God, how I prize your thoughts!

How many of them there are!

18 If I count them, there are more than grains of sand;

if I finish the count, I am still with you.

True love comes only from Him. He will never leave me nor forsake me.

I have learned so much about Gods love, grace and mercy. My parents were entrusted by God to care for me.

Their success and failures are not my concern they are between them and God. Forgiveness is my concern and I not only forgave them but I asked for forgiveness too.

Obedience is better than sacrifice this is what THE Bible tells me and I believe it with my whole heart.

In my obedience to God my dad quit drinking and smoking, and eventually asked Jesus into his heart!

My step-mom is a thousand times better than what she was and God has changed the way I see her. We are very close and God has healed our past. I love her more than even I could imagine it possible to love.

After all these years they are still married and growing old together. No matter what problems they went through I am proud they have gone through they have honored their vows they made with God and I am thankful because I have watched the Lord perform some mighty miracles not just in their daily life but in their health also.

I love my family so very much!

My biological mom and I talk regularly and she asked Jesus in her heart in 2012 and since has

been on fire and Holy Ghost filled and got baptized!

My daughter also got saved and baptized in 2012. She is not fully where she needs to be with God but like my Dad never gave up praying for me, I too not giving up in praying for her.

My son, strayed so far away and I to this day don't know where he is but then again God does and I am not giving up on God to intervene in his life as He did in mine. So I will continue praying in Faith and Hope of what God will do in their lives in His perfect time!

In reality God did answer my childhood prayers...

He healed my family and he has given me a new life and a new name.

And best of all I don't have to run anymore.

I spent my whole life running away from pain

just to run into the arms of the devil when all along my daddy in heaven had his arms wide open ready to catch me and help me.

Today me and my husband "the Crazy Preacher" spend our days on the streets ministering -praying for-loving on the lost and leading them to the Cross of Calvary.

We spent many years operating a full-time residential men and women's faith-based ministry program helping others that come from a lot of the same things I myself and my husband came out of and some even worse situations.

God carried us from there to Pastoring a community outreach church for over a year and now God has moved us back to full time street ministry, evangelism, book writing, going in

and ministering in the schools with the task force and D.A.R.E. team about not drinking and not bullying and wherever He is leading we are going to follow with all faith!!

You see God keeps leading us from season to season in new adventures. It never has been about us directly... it has and is and always will be about God and what Jesus did for us and for our purpose to be fulfilled.

In June of this year, God is doing a new thing in me and a new season. He is bringing up Elisha's to help in carry the load in the ministry and God is taking me through a ministry of writing books and I am starting back to school for my doctorate and PHD in Naturopathic Medicine. I currently help others achieve better health as a personal trainer and nutrition specialist. It is a great move of God to be a part of when He moves us from season to season. We were never meant to get stagnate and stay still. We were meant to stand fast in the liberty of Christ.

Through the week we feed thousands of people in some of the poorest counties from Southeast Missouri to Northeast Arkansas. We don't remain still. We go where God speaks for us to go and where He positions us to be even if it is for a short time.

Time, ALL TIME, belongs to God.

We live and serve by faith not by sight.

God gave me a word for you.

God has requirements of FAITH.

Freedom in the liberty of Christ

Activate your walk and step out

Incline your ear always to the Lord

Trust Him and surrender everything to Him

Hope in His promises (He is no respecter of persons) (He is with wherever you go)

We are the living evidence of a real God. We are evidence that we didn't get here by chance or evolution. We were created by Him, for Him and with Purpose.

Never forget who you belong to.

If you don't know how to have this relationship Him and want to

then turn the page...

GOD'S PLAN OF SALVATION

Becoming a Christian

• To become a Christian a person must first realize that he or she is "lost" – totally estranged from God, separated from God by a sinful nature. Locate a Bible, the history of God's relationship with humankind, and read from the chapter titled Romans.

Romans 3:23: For all have sinned and come short of the glory of God.

• A person alone cannot reconcile the lost relationship between himself or herself and God. To provide a remedy, God sent his only Son, Jesus, to live the perfect life God demands.

Romans 6:23: For the wages of sin is death; but the gift of God is eternal life through Jesus Christ our Lord.

• Although humanity through sin has separated itself from God, the sacrifice of Jesus on the cross bridged that gap.

Romans 5:8: But God commendeth his love toward us, in that while we were yet sinners,

Christ died for us.

• All that God asks is that a man or woman repent of his or her sins, turn from them and accept the sacrifice Christ made on the cross for those sins.

Romans 10:9: That if thou shalt confess with thy mouth the Lord Jesus, and shalt believe in thine heart that God hath raised him from the dead, thou shalt be saved.

• God promises in the Bible that anyone who accepts Jesus as Lord shall be saved.

Romans 10:13: For whosoever shall call upon the name of the Lord shall be saved.

The way we call upon Him is through prayer:

"Dear Lord Jesus, I know that I am a sinner. I also know that you died on the cross for my sins and that you were raised up from the dead. I turn from self and sin and trust you to be my Savior and Lord. Take control of my life and help me to be the person that you want me to be. Save me now and save me forever. Thank you, Lord, for hearing my prayer and saving my soul. In Jesus name, Amen."

Jesus Loves you
and
you are important
to God

ABOUT THE AUTHOR

My name is Jaimie Tipton at the time of writing, I am 53 years old and love writing about what God has done in me and my life. I love giving the testimony that he may receive Glory.

For me and my husband we remain faithful on the streets doing ministry or wherever God carries us to.

If you would more information about our ministry or would like to sow into it please feel free to reach out to us. We are a 501c3 Non-Profit public Charity and all donations are tax deductible.

We are evangelist and are available to come and bring a word to your church.

My husband and I are also ordained minister's. I am lead Speaker for women's conferences so if you would like me to come minister to the women please contact me. Our calendar fills up quickly so please contact us at least 3 months in advance

Tim & Jaimie Tipton

Holy Ghost Outreach Ministries Inc.,
PO Box 250
Ellington, MO 63638
573-210-8466

WEBSITES:
https://hgofitness.wixsite.com/8466

E-MAIL:
#1 e-mail:hg_outreach@yahoo.com
#2 e-mail hgofitness@gmail.com

FACEBOOK:
www.facebook.com/myhgo
www.facebook.com/hgofitness

FINAL THOUGHTS & UPCOMING BOOKS!

Thank you again for sowing into Gods Kingdom!

Be on the lookout for my next book: "For Such a Time As This"

Made in the USA
Columbia, SC
25 October 2021